FLY AWAY FEAR

The Self-help Series

Professor Robert Bor (Series Editor)
Chartered Psychologist and Registered Psychotherapist
Royal Free Hospital
London

FLY AWAY FEAR

OVERCOMING YOUR FEAR OF FLYING

*ELAINE ILJON FOREMAN
AND LUCAS VAN GERWEN*

KARNAC

First published in 2008 by
Karnac Books Ltd
118 Finchley Road, London NW3 5HT

British Library Cataloguing in Publication Data

A C.I.P. for this book is available from the British Library

ISBN: 978 1 85575 580 2

Edited, designed and produced by The Studio Publishing Services Ltd
www.publishingservicesuk.co.uk
e-mail: studio@publishingservicesuk.co.uk

www.karnacbooks.com

Contents

Acknowledgement

Grateful acknowledgement is given for the considerable assistance provided by: Captain T. W. Cummings, Freedom from Fear of Flying Inc., 2021 Country Club Prado, Coral Gables, Florida 33134, USA.

About the Authors

Elaine Iljon Foreman is a Chartered Clinical Psychologist who specializes in the treatment of fear of flying and other anxiety-related problems. She holds an Honours Degree from Durham University, a Master's Degree from Aberdeen University, and is an Associate Fellow of the British Psychological Society. Her highly specialized Freedom to Fly™ treatment programme for fear of flying is based on over twenty years of clinical experience, and on her ongoing research and development of cognitive behaviour therapy. Elaine has carried out her research in conjunction with NHS service provision, as Consultant Clinical Psychologist, specializing in Cognitive Behaviour Therapy. She has researched the treatment of anxiety at Middlesex Hospital Medical School London, and at Aberdeen University. Lectures and workshops are given on an ongoing basis to both professional and self-help audiences. As well as being an invited expert on radio and TV programmes, and having published extensively in the field, her research results have been presented at international conferences in Europe, North America, the Far East, and Australia.

Lucas van Gerwen is a clinical psychologist, psychotherapist, and a professional pilot. As a European registered aviation psychologist, he is Director of the VALK

Foundation, a collaborative venture between the University of Leiden, KLM Royal Dutch Airlines, Transavia Airline, and Amsterdam Airport Schiphol, to help people overcome their fear of flying. He has worked in this field for more than twenty years. The main goals of the VALK Foundation are: to help prevent a fear of flying; to provide a facility for helping those affected overcome their fears and to work with other organizations to develop their own programmes. Together with the University of Leiden, he conducts research into fear of flying, passenger behaviour, and psychological problems among passengers, and for this he received his PhD. He is one of the organizers and the founding father of the International World Conferences on Fear of Flying. Dr van Gerwen is the author of several books on the topic of fear of flying and has published numerous papers in scientific journals on the assessment and treatment of the problem.

To all those who have suffered from fear of flying.
May the sky no longer be the limit.

Foreword to the Series and Title

Therapy has progressed significantly over the past hundred years or so since Freud described a theory of how the mind operates, how human behaviour can be understood, and psychopathology treated. The notion that an outside expert, such as a psychologist, psychotherapist, counsellor, or psychoanalyst, is best placed to help people to identify and resolve their personal problems, has, however, dominated therapy throughout the past century. The results of modern psychological research and patterns observed in contemporary clinical practice have yielded a clearer and deeper understanding of how psychological problems are generated and maintained for a wide range of life's difficulties. With this understanding comes new insights into how people change and how best to treat psychological problems.

The patient's own role in change has, until recently, been under-appreciated. Modern approaches to therapy are marked by a collaborative relationship between therapist and patient, where the patient undertakes some of the work that helps to generate change, alongside the therapist. Self-help should not been misconstrued to mean that the patient undertakes all of this effort on his or her own. Furthermore, simplifying therapy and working collaboratively is not akin to trivializing psychological problems or the personal distress that may accompany these. The therapist is still a vital presence and source of expertise to the patient. However, contemporary therapeutic approaches emphasize how the patient him or herself can be mobilized psychologically and pointed in the right direction to learn more about what maintains his or her problem and to how best to overcome it.

Patients increasingly have access to the Internet, books, self-help manuals, and support groups, where their own efforts to treat their problem can be a significant boost to the effectiveness of many face-to-face therapies. Karnac Books, the leading publishers in the field of mental health, recognize both the importance and relevance of self-help in psychological treatment and readily agreed to publish a series of books that address specific psychological problems.

The first book in this series, *Fly Away Fear: Overcoming Your Fear of Flying*, addresses one of the most common problems experienced by many people in both developed and developing countries. Elaine Iljon Foreman and Lucas van Gerwen, both leading specialists in this field, stress in this book that a fear of flying can profoundly affect people's personal lives, careers, and livelihoods, and yet it is a problem that is highly amenable to psychological treatment. The content of this lively and encouraging book can help fearful flyers to learn an enormous amount about the nature of their fear and how to clinically assess it, and sets out self-help methods for overcoming it.

As the editor for this series of self-help books, it gives me great pleasure to introduce this highly practical and entertaining title. This book will prove to be a valuable tool for those who experience a fear of flying, as well as their families and friends who accompany them on their real and therapeutic journeys. It will also appeal to therapists who work with patients who seek help from them for this problem.

Robert Bor, DPhil, CPsychol, CSci,
FBPsS, UKCP Reg FRAeS
Chartered Psychologist and
Registered Psychotherapist
Royal Free Hospital
London

Introduction and
Questionnaire 1

Most kids are fond of flying, often seeing it as exciting and
even 'cool'. At an early age, they will often point enthusi-
astically towards the sky with a small finger, if a plane
appears. Children are often fascinated by flying and everything to do with it; and they rarely have a fear of flying.
Until the age of around six, that is. Following this time,
the development of a fear of flying becomes more common.

Research indicates that about thirty-five people in
every 100 develop a fear of flying at some point in their
life. Almost everyone knows someone who has it. If you
have ever mentioned to others that you are not comfortable with air travel, you have probably already discovered
just how common is the fear of flying. At social gatherings, celebrations, business functions, or discussions at
work, many people will, albeit reluctantly, admit that
flying is not exactly their favourite form of travel. But it is
not only a bit uncomfortable for some people – the problem can really interfere with their life. It can limit the
choice of holiday destinations, and using other forms of
transport can mean that it takes much longer and is more
costly to get to places that are easily accessible by plane. It
can also interfere with promotion prospects, if this means
that flying is required for a more senior position in one's
chosen field.

Fortunately, the subject is no longer taboo. People will confess more freely that flying is not their preferred mode of transport. And with that brave admission, the first step has been taken towards reclaiming their freedom of movement, because then something can be done to conquer the fear of flying.

Fear of flying is a condition that merits proper attention, and which we are increasingly in a better position to deal with, particularly thanks to clinical research. We now know that fear of flying is similar to other phobias, and that it cannot be dismissed simply as fear of the unknown, and that telling some one to 'pull yourself together' just is not likely to be an effective way to deal with the problem.

There are many identified points as to when and how the fear can first develop.

It may be a result of an unpleasant or frightening experience on a plane – an emergency either for the plane or another passenger. Alternatively, it may be caused by experiencing severe turbulence, or by seeing in a film how flying terrifies others. Maybe one of your parents was afraid of flying. Reading or watching media coverage of an air crash, or seeing a disaster movie, and identifying too closely with the people involved can sometimes be a trigger. Fear of flying can also start when you are flying to a destination to which you do not want to go, or if you have an unpleasant experience just before the flight, or if you have a panic attack, and experience a feeling of impending doom, which then remains associated with everything to do with flying. Having a panic attack before flying, or on an aeroplane, can mean that the person becomes afraid of a repeat experience, and so a pattern of anticipation of feeling anxious and avoidance of flying can begin. However, a considerable number of people say that they noticed that there was no specific trigger, just that over the years, and the more they flew, they found that they became increasingly uncomfortable and even frightened. Far from practice making perfect, they add that the more they flew, the worse it became. There are several theories as to why the incidents mentioned above can lead to a development of a fear of flying in some people, but not in others, and these will be covered in greater detail in this book.

Here are two different examples of the development, taken from the thousands of people we have seen.

Alison is a lady in her thirties. She flew frequently, completely confidently, as a child and in the years before she got married. Financial pressures put paid to holidays by air for a number of years. Having finally saved up sufficient funds to go on a family holiday to Disneyworld, the last thing she expected was what happened to her. When she got on to the plane, she felt overwhelmed by panic, and suffered an overpowering feeling of impending doom. Every catastrophe she had ever read came into her head, and it was all she could do to force herself to stay on the plane, trying hard not to cry, as she did not want to frighten her children. The whole holiday was overshadowed by the dread of the return journey. On her return, despite a completely smooth and trouble-free trip, she vowed she would never fly again.

Peter, aged forty-eight, said he had always been uneasy about flying, but had made himself travel on planes. Whenever he could, he restricted his flights to the shortest possible duration, and the minimum frequency. On one flight, severe, unexpected turbulence was experienced – coffee splashed over his trousers, and cabin crew struggled to their seats. This flight ended with a particularly bumpy landing, and Peter decided he could no longer continue putting himself through what he felt was such an unpleasant, even dangerous experience. He therefore made the return journey by boat, and had not flown until finally, when he retired, he decided he wanted to regain the choice and freedom he had lost, and to overcome his fears, so that he could make the most of the rest of his life.

The list of things that people with a fear of flying say they worry about is very long. It includes: crashing, heights, instability or turbulence, panicking, lack of control, bad weather, suffocation, loss of control in social situations, vomiting or fainting and the subsequent humiliation, worrying what others may think of them, agoraphobia, being trapped in an enclosed space, being separated from a caretaker, experiencing a serious disorder such as a heart attack or brain haemorrhage, 'going mad', experiencing a variety of unpleasant physical sensations, and, of course, the ultimate fear – that of dying.

Though at first sight this looks like a very mixed picture of completely different fears, the bottom line seems to be a fear of loss of control. The fears can be divided into two groups, with just a few people experiencing fears from both groups. The first group are those people who worry about a 'loss of internal control'. These include all those fears about social anxiety, panic disorder, claustrophobia and agoraphobia, and all the other awful feelings. In this first group, the person fears some form of internal catastrophe, where in some way they will go 'out of control'. As they are unable to escape from the situation – leaving at 30,000 feet is just not an option – they remain terrified of the frightening prospect that any second they will be overwhelmed by these seemingly unbearable feelings. The second group fear a 'loss of external control' – something happening to the plane. Their fears include heights, turbulence, bad weather, take-off, landing, and just 'being up there', plus all the factors particularly associated with crashing. They know that if something does go very badly wrong, there is nothing they can do about it, as in reality they have no control over what happens to the plane. The third and smallest group have both fears – a loss of internal and of external control.

The problem can affect people of all ages. Some say they have had the fear for as long as they can remember. They also often mention that they have never been particularly adventurous in other areas of their life, and even sometimes somewhat timid. Others describe it as a difficulty that develops after years of worry-free air travel. This is often the case for people who would see themselves as extroverts who are very much in control of their lives, and who normally have been able to tackle and solve most problems by confronting and overcoming them. Women quite frequently say that it developed after the birth of their first child – suddenly there is someone for whom they are responsible, who depends heavily on them, and the risk of harm coming to them, or their child, must be minimized at all costs.

People may try relaxation, deep breathing techniques, hypnosis, homoeopathy, aromatherapy, medication, or even alcohol to deal with their problems. While these strategies can take the edge off the fear, as 'stand alone' treatments, they do not always prove sufficient to fully overcome it – they just make it seem more bearable. The person still usually dreads the run up to the flight, and then can be very distressed by having to live through the final countdown to the dreaded return flight. The latter fear can sadly tarnish the holiday, taking the shine off it, or can impair one's work performance, giving overseas colleagues a poorer impression of one's abilities than really is the case. It cannot be doubted that people with a flying phobia are entitled to treatment, as are those with any other phobia that cramps activities or takes the joy out of life, and the problem clearly cannot be dismissed as a 'luxury complaint'. Gaining your freedom to expand your enjoyment of life is the purpose of the book you are holding. The book covers a number of areas, including valuable information about flying and everything to do with flying safety. We also cover the nature of anxiety, frequently asked questions, and, of course, the self-help strategies that you can employ. In addition, we deal with professional therapeutic help, and what you can expect of such treatment. We hope that by reading this book you will be less anxious about stepping into an aircraft and that you will experience the flight in a positive way, as an enjoyable and interesting event, which takes you to where you want to be in your life. In our clinical practice, we have seen thousands of people who have successfully overcome their fear, and it is likely that you can do so too!

We would like to thank all the people who have contributed to this book, particularly all those 'formerly fearful flyers' whom we have been able to help overcome their problem, and through whom we have gained considerable insight into the understanding of this highly distressing and limiting problem. We hope you will be able to identify with some of the examples, and to feel that 'If they can do it, so can I!'

Self-evaluation: questionnaire 1

Here is a short questionnaire to see where you are at this point in your flying experience. You will be able to compare this to your responses at the end of the book. We trust the results will speak for themselves!

Fill out the following questionnaire before you continue reading this book. Select the appropriate number on the scale for each question. Be honest and show yourself how you currently deal with flying, and how informed you are about the following subjects.

At the end of this book you will find the same questionnaire repeated, and you can see what has changed.

Not at all————————————Considerably
(0)   (5)

1. How many flights are you planning in the next three years?
   0——1——2——3——4——5

2. How well informed are you about how a plane flies?
   0——1——2——3——4——5

3. How well informed are you about the safety of flying?
   0——1——2——3——4——5

4. How well informed are you about the nature and effects of turbulence?
   0——1——2——3——4——5

5. How well informed are you about the nature and effects of anxiety?
   0——1——2——3——4——5

6. How well informed are you about coping strategies to conquer fear of flying?

   0——1——2——3——4——5

7. How comfortable are you with flying?

   0——1——2——3——4——5

CHAPTER ONE

WHAT'S IT ALL ABOUT?

If only I could fly away fear!

I thought I'd never make it in time! So many things to do before I can leave, and then the desperate scramble of last minute midnight packing – WHERE did I put my passport? Finally I dash to the airport to set off on that well-earned holiday at last. Approaching the airport, I see a jumbo jet taking off. How can something that heavy get up and stay up there? Surely gravity always wins? In my too-vivid imagination I see the catastrophe. Mid-air collision, engine failure, wings falling off, terrorism, sudden severe weather – the list of possibilities is endless. 'It could happen so easily,' I think. And while I know all about flying being the safest form of travel, the feeling is that I am the proverbial cat with nine lives . . . and this is my tenth flight! Panic rises, I feel my mouth go dry and bile rises in my throat. My thoughts race on. 'If my heart beats any faster, I'll surely have a heart attack! Why am I putting myself through this? Though I am going out as a passenger, what will it be like on the return? It's not just that I'll feel trapped, once those doors close and we take off – I really am! And there'll be nothing I can do about it!'

Determinedly, I resist the temptation to just turn around and forget the whole thing. All that bustle at the check-in desk, those long queues, and how can everyone be so unconcerned? Don't they know what fate awaits them? Superstitious thoughts assail me – black cats, magpies, ladders, salt over which shoulder? Of course the staff can smile and joke – they aren't getting on my plane!

Sitting next to a mother and baby momentarily reassures me – this must mean it's safe, as what parent would risk their child's life? 'Cabin crew, take your seats,' I hear over the intercom. Here we go. We are ready for take-off. There's no escape now. I clutch at the armrests, white knuckled, all the while attempting to sit 'lightly' on my seat. When the plane banks, I find myself leaning in the opposite direction to compensate. Each change in engine sound provokes the heart-stopping thought of engine failure, while the slightest bump feels unbearable. If only I could open the window!

Breaking through the clouds, and seeing the blue sky and sunshine, I momentarily appreciate the beauty, but this is soon lost in the awful anticipation, waiting for the next bump or noise to remind me how vulnerable I am. I find myself thinking, 'If man was meant to fly . . .'

All the statistics in the world can't convince me: after all, remember the lottery advert, 'It could be YOU!' There's nothing statistical about my fear. Despite the odds, I feel much safer with tarmac under my wheels than with miles of gaping void underneath me! [Taken from the confessions of a former flying phobic]

How limiting is your fear?

To which of these groups do you belong? Internationally, up to 40% of people say they are or have been afraid of flying. They range from those who have never flown before, to frequent flyers, and also include both civilian and military aircrew. Some who have never flown before say they would never want to, while others used to fly, either confidently or with fear, but then reached the point of total avoidance. A final group continue to fly, but with great trepidation, keeping their trips as short and as infrequent as possible.

If you or someone close to you does suffer from this fear, you probably already know that the consequences can be far-reaching, limiting professional opportunities, affecting leisure options, even to the extent that one person may decide to take holidays without their partner on a regular basis, if the partner will not fly. There are implications for long-term relationships, and likewise difficulties in family holidays if children refuse to travel. The problem can, therefore, have a substantial affect on one's professional, social, and family life, given the way in which it hampers or restricts either partner's freedom of movement.

Take the example of Sylvia, who finally decided that it was time to overcome her fear. Sylvia describes her experience in the following manner.

> Are you scared of flying? I was, but it was much more than that. I even refused to get myself a passport, as that meant I was definitely unable to go abroad. You see, flying was only one aspect of my fears. During my early years it did not matter, as I had neither the time nor money to go abroad on holiday. Holidays in the UK were great – good venues – good countryside – plenty to do. But expensive. However, as time progressed some of these reasons for not flying began to wear thin, and began to appear no longer sufficiently valid for not going abroad.

3

Friends tried to encourage me, telling me about all sorts of exciting places I could go to. Places I could see, and experience, instead of merely watching them on TV. To tell the truth, I didn't even really enjoy seeing those travel programmes or talking to the friends who assured me that real life was far better! Then my nephew and family thought they might emigrate: 'Only to Australia!' he said, 'You'll be able to visit!' No passport! Scared of flying! The other end of the earth? 'No way!' I thought.

Let me explain further: flying was only one aspect of my fears. I was unable to drive a car up higher than the third floor of a multi-storey car park. I was unable to go down the escalators in all those modern shopping centres. I did not like lifts, and so it continued. Oh! By the way, did I mention that I was in my fifties (early), a difficult time of life to let people know you are scared?!

Then a number of things happened. I told my friends to stop hassling me to go abroad. This was a pressure I did not need. I phoned one of the national airports and asked if they knew of a Fear of Flying course. They gave me two telephone numbers. One for a national airline, who had vacancies in about three months' time. I then phoned the second number, which was that of Freedom to Fly, who said they could offer me a place in ten days time.

I stood holding the phone and shaking – what had I done? Until then I had only confessed my problems to a very few friends, in order not to have to explain myself to too many others and thus increase the pressure. Now I was really terrified! What *had* I done?!

Sylvia's story is typical of so many people's experience. Perhaps you have a fear of flying; if not, do you know someone who does? Think about the difficulties, and how they fit with the finding that, as mentioned in the introduction, fears can be seen as falling into those two types of loss of control. They are either about a fear of a loss of external control – something happening to the plane – that you are helpless to do anything about. This includes worries about the plane crashing and the fearful person dying as a result. Turbulence, heights, bad weather, and flying over water can be aspects of this fear of loss of external control.

Or perhaps you are one of those people who are afraid of a loss of internal control. This can mean being afraid, like Alison and Sylvia, of having a panic attack, either before take-off or in the air. You find yourself sweating, shaking, and having palpitations, which can make you feel as if you are going to faint or even have a heart attack. Perhaps you worry about making a fool of yourself in front of others, or even losing control of your bodily functions and messing yourself. If you suffer from claustrophobia, you may even be concerned that you might be overwhelmed by panic and feel compelled to open the door during the flight, although you know that you cannot really open it, given the higher pressure in the plane. Agoraphobia – a fear of being away from home or a place of safety can also be seen as one of the elements in a fear of a loss of internal control. Perhaps you fear that something catastrophic will happen to you if you cannot get away, and escape to a place of safety. You also may worry that if something does happen, you will never be able to return home.

If we look at these fears in more detail, the linking with a fear of flying becomes clearer. It is important to recognize that everything we do in life carries some degree of risk. Accidents certainly do happen, and so it is only logical that even flying, arguably the safest form of transport, can never be 100% safe either. Unexpected jolts can give us a fright, and every aircraft occasionally jolts without warning. You have control only over yourself, not over the plane or the weather – while the pilot controls the one, Providence the other. If you are the sort of person who wants to keep control over everything in your daily life, always insisting on driving yourself, even tending to control others, you are possibly going to have a difficult time in an aircraft, where you have to leave the control to other people.

A commercial aircraft generally cruises at an altitude of 30,000 feet, or 9–12 kilometres. If you suffer from a fear of heights, this may seem impossibly high. And yet there are some people who suffer from a fear of heights, but who feel perfectly comfortable in an aircraft, as they say it is very different from being high up but still connected to the ground, for instance on a balcony or a mountainside. Many pilots admit to a fear of heights – not for the world could they be persuaded to go up on a ladder and clean out their own roof gutter, but they have no qualms about flying at 35,000 feet up in the sky. Perhaps you are one of those passengers for whom a fear of heights only really makes itself felt if you sit beside the window, or when the aircraft banks into a turn and you realize how far above the earth you're hanging. Though you are afraid of heights, you might even ask for a window seat, just to make sure that the blind stays down whenever possible!

Looking at the problem of claustrophobia, there are people who cannot bring themselves to enter a lift, or who never lock the toilet door, because they cannot endure the thought of being shut in. Such fear is similarly liable to make itself felt in an aircraft, which, after all, is an enclosed space. Considering fears relating to water and swimming, somebody who travels blithely overland by car, bus, or train, but fears being on a boat, will probably feel more than a little nervous in an aircraft crossing a wide expanse of water. Fear of the dark can also be a factor in the fears, as flying is done by night as well as by day. In an aircraft, it is possible to switch on your own overhead light, but, in the air as on the ground, this may not be enough to dispel fear of the encircling blackness. Finally, there is fear of crowds. If you are somebody who avoids cinemas, theatres, football matches, and other gatherings because you cannot abide being thrown together with a herd of strangers, you are liable to have problems with flying, where the point of departure is usually a crowded airport terminal, and the aircraft itself seems like a room full of strangers.

As can be seen, there are a considerable number of different fears which can also be experienced by people who are afraid of flying, and these fears encompass many elements. On the plus side, considering what can happen when one has successfully overcome one's fears, many people report that they have been able to use the therapeutic techniques learned in the treatment of their fear of flying to conquer other difficulties. This liberation can in many cases open up a new world to former sufferers, literally and metaphorically.

So, fear of flying is no 'luxury complaint' – it is a pressing problem that demands a solution. Getting rid of it is likely to make your life a whole lot easier and more pleasant, in all sorts of ways, and not just when you have to fly.

Emma, a lady from London, aged 47, commented, 'The treatment has changed my life in so many ways. I was never a very confident person, but having actually done it and mastered it, I feel there other things I could do. It's given me more confidence in myself, what I can do once I have decided I am going to do it!'

Henry, from Kent, aged 69, said of his previously widespread travel fears, 'There's nothing I won't go on or do now. It's a different form of transport, but exactly the same situation and approach.'

And then there was Robert, who, describing the difference, said, 'I've completely turned everything around. Through conquering my fear of flying, I've conquered everything else that I feared. It's just the fact that you have to look at everything logically and I'm doing that in my whole life now.'

What causes fear of flying

There are many different theories as to the cause. In searching for agreement on what fear of flying really is, it is interesting to consider that, in the very early years, a reluctance to fly was regarded as a completely normal human attitude. Looking at the formal classification, the current medical definition now says that this problem is

> characterized by a marked, persistent, excessive fear that is precipitated by the experience or immediate prospect of air travel. Exposure to this phobic stimulus almost invariably provokes an anxiety response – sometimes to the point of a panic attack – which the individual recognises as unreasonable, and which produces significant interference or distress.

Can you recognize yourself, or someone you know, in this definition?

There are many different theories as to the underlying causes of the fear. Some writers suggest there are 'internal, unconscious processes and mechanisms behind the fears'. Freud's writing also suggests an underlying cause, where the plane represents something else with which the person has a problem. Other writers say that the fears are conditioned – having had a frightening time, one automatically experiences anxiety on re-entering a similar situation, or even when just thinking about it. There is also the view that, after an unpleasant experience, the person starts to avoid the situation, and so never learns that a repeat occurrence is unlikely.

Another way of understanding the problem is to consider that the fear of flying might actually represent a difficulty in communication. Refusing to fly can be seen as expressing a different message – for instance that a child does not want to return to boarding school, or that a partner resents being uprooted yet again to follow their spouse's promotion trail. Developing a fear of flying can enable the problem in communication within the relationship to go unchallenged. It is also interesting to consider the nature of the language in use at airports – 'last and final call' for a particular flight, a flight 'terminating' at its 'final destination', – the airport 'terminal' and the 'departure' lounge. All of these do very little to reassure the nervous flyer.

The different theories point towards different treatments – from the possibility of years of psychotherapy to try to understand the 'underlying problem' to learning ways to change your thoughts and behaviour to enable you to confront your difficulties and speedily overcome them.

Who develops the fear?

It has been suggested that flying phobia develops in people who are more vulnerable to events that may have had little effect on others. So, while some people can just shrug something off, if others are going through a tough time, and are more sensitive to such experiences, they may find that they cannot do so. The reasons why some people are more susceptible to particular stresses at particular times than are others, are probably partly acquired and partly inborn. To the extent that they are acquired, what is especially important is the way in which people with a lower stress tolerance – or who are more anxious – learn how to deal with stressful situations. So, someone who easily becomes stressed, but who has learned particular coping techniques, including how to relax as much as possible in stressful situations, can eventually build up a greater tolerance to such situations than someone with the same tendencies who has not learned such techniques. In a similar way, if you are an anxious individual who has learned to talk about your anxiety with someone else (even if only briefly) it is likely that you will be able to deal more easily with the situation than a similarly anxious person who 'bottles up' the anxiety.

The latter run the risk of becoming so preoccupied with a variety of fearful thoughts and ideas that they lose sight of the real situation, becoming impervious to any reasoning, explanation, or information. Someone who reacts in this way may well, in the long run, baulk at flying altogether, perhaps insisting on getting off the plane even when it has just started to move. Alternatively, they may find that the only way to cope is by using alcohol or tranquillizers in order to try to suppress the frightening thoughts and feelings.

Not all anxious individuals try to avoid experiencing their uncomfortable feelings. Some people specifically look out for the things that may make them anxious, and this has been called 'monitoring' the situation. If the person is worried about something happening to them physically, and continuously takes their pulse rate, an increase in heart rate could well trigger more anxiety, and an even higher heart rate. Other people can try to cope using techniques such as distraction and avoidance of talking about their fears ('DON'T THINK ABOUT IT!!!'). These are known as 'Bluntors'. Once again, the coping techniques can lead to the exact opposite of the desired effect – the more one tries not to think about something, the more one's mind insists on focusing on it.

There is yet another element that can be a factor in making someone susceptible to a fear of flying: perfectionism. Perfectionists impose high standards on themselves and others. For this reason, they often find it difficult to accept the situation where they themselves react fearfully to certain situations – such as flying – but where other people have no difficulties. They may have trouble accepting something they see as a 'psychological flaw' in their own character, and judge themselves severely for it, but the only result of their anger with themselves is that they become even more stressed.

As previously mentioned, it is quite frequently the case that after having had a child, a woman may be more likely to develop a fear of flying. While her life has always been important, having a child means that she is now responsible for someone who is extremely dependent on her. She can find herself worrying about harm that may befall her,

11

and how that would affect her child. She also does not want to be responsible for exposing her child to danger. The risks one is prepared to take can change as one grows older – we are all familiar with 'tearaway teenager' behaviour, and some people say they shudder to think what they got up to when they were young, and wonder how they got away with it!

In a similar vein, men and women describe the fear as gradually creeping up as they became older. It is as if when one is young one feels invincible and immortal, but with age comes the knowledge that statistically one is getting nearer to the end of one's life, and one therefore tries to delay, and certainly is in no hurry to speed up, this process.

Often, disturbed sleep can be a factor in the development of the problem. Tiredness and being 'run down' can make it more likely that a problem will develop. People then start to worry about not sleeping – only to find that sleep becomes even more elusive! It is also common for a person who is going through a stressful time in their life – bereavement, illness, involvement in an unrelated traumatic event such as a car accident, problems at work or in relationships – to find that thy become more anxious and 'worked up'. This heightened state of arousal can mean that they are more likely to develop a fear of flying at this point in their life.

Another factor is one that, while it does not cause fear of flying, can help to maintain it once the fear has become established. Like all other fears, fear of flying can sometimes have a positive side to it. For instance, an overburdened executive who frequently has to fly may find some relief from the workload if permitted to travel less often because of a phobia about flying. The projects requiring flying may then be taken over by a colleague, and so there is a certain benefit from the fear. It is also possible that someone with flying phobia may receive extra attention from family and friends in the days before he or she has to fly. Those people are sorry to see someone so distraught, and try their best to help by being kind and helpful. All this attention would not be received if it was not for the fear of flying, and in some cases the motivation to finally get rid of this fear may be greatly reduced. However, for most people, in the long run the disadvantages of flying phobia seriously outweigh the advantages (if any), and those affected really do suffer greatly as a result of the problem.

The problem in a nutshell

It is generally agreed that it is not the actual events, but rather how one makes sense of them that causes such feelings as anxiety and/or depression. This is clearly put in the following quote from Epictetus, a philosopher who lived from *c.* 55–135 AD. He said, 'People are disturbed not by events, but by the view they take of them.'

When one is anxious, one tends to have an exaggerated perception of danger. Things that did not worry one in the past, such as changes in engine noise, suddenly become signals that something terrible is about to happen. It is not only the outside events that are seen as a source of danger, but also what is happening inside the person – the normal physical sensations that someone experiences when feeling anxious – makes them feel as if they really are in danger. The two elements then become linked, so that once someone has labelled a situation as dangerous,

13

they tend to selectively scan and interpret other situations in ways that magnifies their sense of being in danger. As will be seen, the Self-Help Techniques are aimed at helping you to break this vicious circle.

Once the problem is seen in this encapsulated form, it then becomes possible to understand that this is just one possible way of interpreting information and events. This new perception opens up a substantial variety of different alternative thoughts and behaviours that were not previously available.

The result of putting one's new alternatives into practice can mean that when you are successful in conquering your fear, then the sky is, in fact, no longer the limit.

CHAPTER TWO

BACK TO BASICS

Safety: the facts

It is worth stressing at this point that the facts alone are unlikely to prove sufficient for someone to overcome completely their fear of flying. This section of the book must therefore be taken as only a part of the wider picture.

Does the number of those suffering from fear for flying reflect the hard figures about flying and security? No, because fear and the probability of danger are not necessarily related in an apparently logical fashion. This can be seen in the story below, looking at the experience of a former fearful flyer.

> When we planned our holiday, I found myself becoming positively excited at the prospect of sunshine, sea and all that wonderful foreign food! However, as the day of departure neared, the further my excitement receded, and I had an increasing realization of the foolishness of our plans. While I knew all about the statistics, still the feeling was 'I know it's one in 10 million – but I also know who that one is going to be! Delaying going to the airport, we were then nearly too late (I should be so lucky!). Somehow we checked in, and I forced myself to board the plane. With hands and feet as cold as icicles, I listened in horrid fascination to what felt like the last sounds I would ever hear. And as for the meal? Who could eat at a time like this?

Despite the laws of aerodynamics, I just cannot believe this huge hunk of metal will really stay up there – with me inside it! I am entirely convinced that this plane remains exclusively and only in the air thanks to my intense efforts of will. At each movement or bump I clutch the seat. The sweat pours off my face. I feel like a rat in a trap. An announcement of impending turbulence makes me whimper. Surely this is the end. I almost wish something terrible would happen, just to put me out of my misery! 'Just relax', I am told. RELAX? You just have to be kidding! 'Please let me make it this time and I promise I'll NEVER do this again!' I vow.

As mentioned above, for the person who is convinced of the danger, statistics alone will not suffice. Their answer is likely to be along the lines of 'If we were meant to fly, we would have been born with wings.' Countering this with 'If man was meant to travel at seventy miles per hour on a motorway, he, like the cheetah, would have been born with spots', is unlikely to provide the desired therapeutic breakthrough necessary to overcome the problem!

A fearful flyer does not evaluate how realistic it is to be frightened of something that could, but seldom does, occur. The American sociologist Barry Glasner carried out research which reached the conclusion that many of the fears, including fear of flying, which concern something terrible happening to the person, are actually about statistically unlikely events. However, it is not the real risk, but our perception of that risk, and, of course, the severity of the consequences if it were to happen, that determines our degree of fear. The way we assess danger influences our behaviour in our private lives, and also affects the decisions that we take at work. The first author was actually on a flight where the Captain's greeting to the passengers began: 'Congratulations, ladies and gentlemen. You have just completed the most dangerous part of your journey – getting to the airport!' Table 1, compiled by the psychologist T. S. Greco on the probability of coming to harm in different situations, makes for fascinating reading.

As can be seen, one has a greater statistical chance of dying if one avoids flying and stays at home, than if one were to take a flight and end up being killed in a plane crash. Given the odds of one in fourteen million to win the UK National Lottery, it is sobering to realize that one is more likely to be dead by the end of the week than to have won the lottery!

Exaggeration of a threat is a typical error made during times of fear. When faced with complex, uncertain situations, it often feels safer to escape or avoid. But putting

Table 1. Danger of flying in relation to other modes of transport or situations in the USA.

Mode of transport/ situation	Number of deaths per year in USA	Comparative safety of airline travel
Car	45,000	29 times safer
Walking/being a pedestrian	8,000	8 times safer
Staying at home	20,000 accidental deaths	18 times safer
Working on the job	11,000 accidental fatalities	10 times safer
Homicide by spouse or relative	7,000 homicides	6 times safer
Bus		4 times safer per mile
Train		4 times safer
Boating		8 times safer

Source: USA Department of Transport Document. Greco.

perception to one side, let us look at the facts when we pose the question, 'How dangerous is flying really?'

In the period from 1990 till 2002, 914 people per year worldwide died as a result of aircraft accidents. In the year 2003, 677 people worldwide died as a result of aircraft accidents, and twenty-five aircraft accidents took place. In the year 2004, 428 people worldwide died as a result of civil aviation aircraft accidents, and twenty-five aircraft accidents took place. Moving on to 2006 and 2007, the number of accidents involving fatalities decreased to twenty per year. The facts show that flying continues to become ever safer, with the number of aircraft accidents decreasing, and also show that for years the figure has been stably low. With the increasing safety, the number of victims has steadily decreased – compare the 597 airline passenger deaths in 2007 *worldwide*, with the road deaths for the UK of 3,172 and the Dutch figure of 1,100 victims in that year. Thus, air transport continues to be the safest form of travel. One further interesting statistic is that the number of US highway deaths in atypical six-month period is about 21,000, which roughly equals all commercial jet fatalities worldwide since the dawn of jet aviation four decades ago!

In spite of the increasing demands on airspace, flying continues to become steadily safer. Of course, there is no means of transport in existence that is 100% safe. It is also understandable that one can feel frightened when one empathizes with the victims. However, as can be seen from the Table 1, above, the conclusion is clear – if we want travel in the safest possible way, then air travel is our best choice. To put it even more strongly, if a person flew around the earth for their entire life, assuming sufficient air, food and water, they would probably live longer than if they stayed on the ground!

It is, however, quite understandable that most people have a distorted view of flying safety. After all, the media mainly focuses on air transport when there's an accident, never mentioning the hundred thousand daily flights that pass without incident – normality is not newsworthy – and so won't sell newspapers! Sometimes we get blanket coverage of the same disaster in the press and on the television for days at a time. Much less attention is paid to road accidents, both because they occur so comparatively frequently that we've become used to them, and because generally fewer people are killed or injured per incident. This is despite the fact that, overall, the number of people killed on the roads is much greater than the number of air accident victims. A newspaper report put it in this way – a fully laden jumbo jet would have to crash every day for a year with no survivors to equal the annual road death toll in the United States. It is ironic, however, that while nothing we do in this life is completely safe, and that includes flying, when aviation safety records are broken, as for example when a particular year is the safest in the post-war history of flying, there is hardly a word about it in the press.

This is unfortunate, because the behaviour of the media is of great importance in shaping people's fears and anxieties. In America, it has been shown that people tend to evaluate particular risks on the basis of the number of words written about that subject in the press. For instance, people in that country tend to strongly overestimate the chances of getting cancer, while underestimating the chances of an asthma attack. While the assertion that flying is safe is easy to illustrate with figures, airline passengers can also take comfort in the fact that insurance companies do not charge higher premiums for flying than they do for trips by car, boat, or train.

When you see a traffic accident you may perhaps think, 'That won't happen to me – I'm a safe driver, and anyway I'm always in control, so if anyone else does something stupid, I can get out of it!' Or you may think that most road traffic accidents are not fatal, and in that you are correct. If you do think, 'That could have been me!', either in relation to the road traffic accident or, indeed, any other potentially dangerous situation, this is likely to affect, at least for a short while, the way you feel and act when faced with a similar situation. But it is also true that in aviation, just as on the road, by far the greatest number of accidents are not fatal, and 96% of passengers survive aircraft accidents. Strangely enough, there are not many people who realize this. Altogether, it is worthwhile considering that all the civilian airlines together carry a total of more than two billion passengers each year. Another way of seeing how safe flying is can be shown by the fact that in the United States and Europe 99.999999% of airline passengers reach their destination safely.

Risk perception, however, is not only influenced by the news media – films can provide a horrifying vicarious experience that can give one nightmares for months. Movies are not constrained by reality, but fantasy can frequently masquerade as the real thing, just to make it more exciting! If you are sensitive to some of the sensational, but often inaccurate, entertainment you are offered, your perception of both risk and its consequences can be influenced. Think of the bad press that *Jaws* gave to seaside holidays!

In short, the figures could not be more comforting. Looking at the USA, more people are killed on the roads in a single day than die as a result of air travel in a whole year, and we would have to add up the average number of airline accident victims over ten years throughout the world to equal the number of fatal accidents that occur in private swimming pools in only one year, according to the US National Transportation Safety Board. However, the fact remains, as stated at the beginning of this chapter, that figures alone cannot banish fear of flying. Certainly the people who are worried about the possibility of crashing are likely to say, 'I know the probability is one in 10 million. Now tell me, WHO is the one?'

So why am I still not convinced?

If flying is so safe – in fact, the safest of all the forms of transport, as we have seen in the previous chapter – why are so many people still afraid of it? The present chapter looks for answers to this question.

Let us start by putting the problem into context. All over the world there are some people who are afraid of various types of transport. Some are afraid of travelling by car, some of boarding a bus or train. There are people who are afraid of making a boat trip, and additionally there are also those who are afraid of flying in an aircraft. 'Transport fears' are, therefore, fairly common internationally. To complete the picture we should add the fears of cycling (motor and pedal) using lifts (both ski lifts and also lifts in buildings), plus underground tube travel, trams, and rickshaws. It is probable that on a worldwide scale, these other forms of 'transport fear' are more common than fear of flying.

Looking at transport fears, for certain people going on a journey and leaving home for any length of time is always accompanied by some degree of anxiety. Leaving or being away from our own familiar environment, which we feel to be safe, can lead to feelings of fear. Other people do not want to trust their lives to 'technology'. Conveyances such as a car, boat, train, lift, or aircraft are technically complicated things, and many people feel that by stepping into them, except perhaps as the driver, they are entrusting their lives to something they do not understand, and to someone they do not know. They think of all sorts of things that could go wrong, and are aware that they have no control over it.

But apart from these factors, other elements can play an important role in fear of flying. The stress that is associated with flying or that occurs during a flight can also be a factor in the development of flying phobia, as can anxieties associated with the journey by air. For example, a twenty-one-year-old girl travelled by air to visit a member of her family, only to learn on arrival that her relative had died. The resulting shock and anguish became associated with flying, and eventually led to a full-blown phobia. In another case, an employee was under pressure to make business trips. He did not feel that his work had the right to dictate what he should do. During one flight, which was far from calm, the fears became stronger, and on his return he vowed that no one would make him fly again. Finally, a lady described how, for all of her married life, her husband had made the decisions of where they would go, when, and for how long. She felt powerless in the relationship, and increasingly dreaded the flights, which took her away from home, where she felt she did at least have some control and say in her life. Gradually, she developed a full-blown phobia, and reached the point where she could not face air travel at all.

For fear of flying to develop as a result of an unpleasant episode, the event responsible does not necessarily have to be something that has actually happened; it can also be as a result of using one's imagination. The second author once treated a woman who had seen an air disaster on the television news, and who identified strongly with one of the victims. When she herself boarded an aircraft not long afterwards, she imagined herself in the place of the victim, and became frightened as a result. Avoidance then followed, the anxiety increased, and so the development of her phobia commenced.

As you can imagine, providing the safety facts alone was not enough to enable these people to change. However, we trust that this book will show you ways of using the safety information, in combination with the exercises and additional understanding provided, and that this will mean that you, like so many of the people we have seen, will be able to overcome your difficulties.

Understanding anxiety and fear

Fear is a reaction to danger, or something that we perceive as dangerous. As such, fear is a very important reaction, and also a very healthy one, since it enables us to recognize and then choose to avoid particular people, situations, or events that we think form a real threat to our life and well-being. However, not only do we live in a world of real, tangible things, situations, and people, but also in a world of symbols, the intangible. We can easily mix up the impressions generated by external stimuli and the impressions that are purely the product of our imagination. For this reason we continually run the risk of experiencing fear due solely to a danger summoned up by our imagination, without being fully aware of the facts.

23

Anxiety is a word that is often used to describe both the physical sensations that accompany fear as well as the thoughts about what is happening to one. As already mentioned, fear is a normal, healthy reaction by our bodies to situations or events that are perceived as threatening, dangerous, or alarming. Our bodies and minds are programmed to react with emergency measures not only to acute threats or problems, but also to situations of great stress or tension. This is the 'flight-or-fight' response. It is accompanied by, among other things, the secretion of certain hormones, such as adrenaline and cortisol, known as stress hormones. These hormones stimulate the liver to convert stored glucose into energy, they speed up breathing and heart rate, and they increase tension in the muscles. In other words, they prepare the body either to stand and fight, or to make a rapid getaway. Both reactions are of vital importance – in some cases literally a matter of life or death.

Consider the case where you are driving your car along a deserted country road. You approach a level crossing that has no gates. You slow down, and while the car bumps over the crossing, the engine falters and then stalls. To your horror, the car remains stuck in the middle of the crossing. You desperately try to restart the engine. The starter motor turns but the engine refuses to catch. All at once, you hear the warning signal of an approaching train. The psychological consequences are easy to guess: wild feelings of panic, and a strong and very sensible urge to get out of the way as quickly as possible. A whole series of violent reactions also occur within your body. There is a rush of adrenaline. Your heartbeat and respiration rates soar. Your muscles tense. Your peripheral blood vessels contract, reducing the flow of blood to your hands and feet and increasing the supply to your muscles. Your liver pours energy into your bloodstream in the form of glucose. Meanwhile, you break out in a sweat. These reactions and the sudden urge to flee are crucial for your chances of escaping unharmed from the situation. The rush of adrenaline and the increased flow of blood to the muscles momentarily give you faster reactions and greater strength, and all your energy is concentrated on escaping. If this didn't happen, you probably would not get away in time. In short, just as occurs in animals, a panic reaction in humans might be a natural, healthy, and extremely useful reaction of the mind and body in response to sudden danger. The operative word, however, is 'might'.

The trouble is that panic reactions – with the same powerful symptoms just described – can also occur when there is no such life-threatening situation. In such a case, we speak of 'spontaneous' panic attacks. These are the type of panic attacks that make you suddenly wake up at night, bathed in sweat, or that strike without warning when you are walking along the street or sitting alone at home. It is exactly the same in terms of physical reactions as the panic reaction that comes over you when you get stuck on a level crossing, or when you surprise burglars in your home. The same applies to a panic attack that hits you when you are sitting in an aircraft flying peacefully through the air, or for that matter during turbulence, which, when you are wearing your seatbelt, is, after all, a question of comfort, not of safety. What makes a spontaneous panic attack so troublesome to deal with is that the violent physical reactions occur without any immediate obvious danger threatening, so you have no idea why these alarming symptoms are happening. And not knowing why makes the experience even more frightening. Human psychology being what it is, our reaction to sudden, intense, and inexplicable feelings is to be frightened by these feelings themselves, and to believe that we are in danger.

Unfortunately, there is no consensus as to why spontaneous panic attacks occur. Some psychologists believe that there always has to be some sort of outside trigger, even if the person suffering the attack is not aware of it. The risk of spontaneous panic attacks is known to be greater in people who are chronically under great stress, or who have recently suffered bereavement. However, only a small proportion of people in these categories develop panic attacks. It is also known that a change in the functioning of a certain brain centre, the locus coeruleus in the brain stem, made up of cells that are very rich in neurotransmitters, can play a role in spontaneous panic attacks. However, this factor is probably only one link in a long chain of all the factors involved.

Spontaneous panic attacks seem to be relatively frequent. According to some studies, three out of ten people have at least one such attack per year. A much smaller number of people, estimated at around one in 100, suffer from 'panic syndrome', which means, among other things, that during the past four weeks they have had at least one (and frequently more) spontaneous panic attacks; that they are very worried about having another attack; and that during an attack they suffer symptoms such as shortness of breath, feelings of suffocation, faintness or dizziness, a pounding heart, shaking or trembling, perspiration, gasping for breath, queasiness or stomach complaints, prickling sensations in their limbs, pain or tightness in the chest, the feeling of 'not being themselves', and fear of dying, going mad, or completely losing control over themselves.

Since, by definition, there is no apparent threat when a spontaneous panic attack occurs, many people tend to see a supposed danger in the violent physical symptoms. The thought pattern tends to be along the lines of 'If I feel so terrible, there must be something dangerous going on. If there is no external danger, the danger must come from inside me.' As a result, people suffering from a panic attack tend to attribute it to one or more dangers such as: 'I'm having a heart attack' or 'I'm dying' (in reaction to a pounding heart); 'I'm suffocating' (in reaction to shortness of breath); 'I'm going to fall over' (in reaction to giddiness); 'I'm going mad' (in reaction to feeling not quite one's self); or 'I'm losing control over myself' (in reaction to the intensity of the physical symptoms). If somebody tells themself this sort of thing when experiencing certain panic symptoms, the panic naturally becomes worse. This in turn causes more panic, so leading to a 'spiral of panic'.

So, as can be seen, worrying about your fear reactions causes greater fear. The physical feelings of fear can themselves be frightening. They can lead to the idea that something is wrong with you – or is going wrong – physically or mentally, and that you are in great danger. This idea exacerbates your feelings of fear, which in turn increases your physical fear reactions, and so on.

Physical reactions

Fear   Increased fear

Stronger physical reactions

To further complicate matters, the concern about your fear reaction to certain situations or events eventually starts to become apparent long before the situation or event actually arises. The expectation – the thought that

27

you will start to become fearful – begins hours, days or even weeks before. In other words, you start to anticipate your own fear. What this boils down to is that you start to become fearful about the fear that you will feel at a certain moment. The problem is that this very fearfulness does actually inspire the fear itself, and this in turn leads into an endless wave of panic.

Fear   Fear of the fear   More fear   More fear of the fear   More fear   etc

It is perfectly normal to avoid dangerous situations. But when the fear starts to become chronic, this usually results in you avoiding situations that are not objectively dangerous. Situations typically avoided by people suffering from panic attacks are busy places such as shops or stations, queues, mixing in groups, or participating in meetings. But meeting other people and going shopping are important and necessary parts of daily life. If you have a tendency to avoid these situations, this will frequently cause inconvenience, which can then lead to problems at work and at home.

Some forms of avoidance are more subtle than others. People may postpone things that they know they will eventually have to do. Others try to stop thinking about things they find difficult, and attempt to ignore the problem. Although avoiding people and situations can bring some relief, it usually does not solve the problem in the long run, since the relief is only temporary. People often feel very angry with themselves for giving in and avoiding, and this anger and frustration can make them feel even more tense. They then are faced with the next inevitable problem, 'How to keep avoiding', and this in turn causes further anxiety and tension. Generally, it is found that the more often you avoid something, the harder it becomes actually to confront it at last, and so the circle frequently expands ever outward as one starts to avoid more and more things, slowly but surely.

Avoiding numerous situations or events eventually erodes your self-confidence. Because it becomes more and more difficult to do things that you previously did without any bother, or those that other people seem to manage perfectly easily, or ones that enable you to fulfil your ambitions, this restriction can make you see yourself as less confident and less able than when you did not have the problem. Linked to that, your self-esteem may also fall.

What is self-confidence? It is the satisfying feeling that comes from doing things well, in the way you want to or would like to be able.

How do we obtain self-confidence? We build it up by doing things and seeing that we do them well. Other people cannot give you self-confidence, because true self-confidence is the product of your own 'success'. Alcohol and medication may give you a temporary feeling of self-confidence, but they generally do not affect the solid inner core on which self-confidence is built. In the long term, regular drug usage can give rise to the problems of tolerance, where you need more and more of the drug to have the same effect, plus potentially developing both physical and psychological dependence.

How do we lose self-confidence? We lose self-confidence when we find that we cannot do the things that we thought we could, or that we used to be able to, or that people in a similar situation can do. We also can lose self-confidence when people in a similar situation in our immediate environment do not show any understanding for things we feel we cannot do.

How do we regain self-confidence? We can regain self-confidence by learning to deal with smaller, less frightening, or less important things, before taking on bigger tasks or challenges.

Later in this book we will describe a number of ways of preventing a panic attack from becoming a panic spiral, such as relaxation and breathing exercises, getting involved in other activities, and thought retraining. With regard to the latter, it should be emphasized once more that a very effective solution is not to interpret the unpleasant physical sensations of panic as heralding some sort of danger or catastrophe. If you constantly repeat (aloud or to yourself) that whatever else they are, sensations in times of anxiety such as dizziness, tightness in the chest, racing heart and the like, are normal, healthy, harmless physical reactions, and not signals of impending danger, then you are likely to eventually have fewer panic attacks, or even none at all.

Let us consider the above specifically in relation to air travel. As has been shown, fear can become a problem if it arises when there is:

1. No objective danger.
2. Danger which is perceived as greater than it is in reality.
3. Fear which continues long after the danger has disappeared.
4. No possibility of either fighting or fleeing.

When there is no objective danger, or when the danger is perceived to be greater than it actually is, the fear can lead to the avoiding of situations or events that present little or no difficulty for most other people. At that moment the fear has become our Dictator. While our children and spouse step on board the plane to their holiday destination without a care in the world, we have to follow by train or car. To make matters worse, we just cannot explain to them why we really do not want to fly.

When the fear continues long after the danger has disappeared, or when there is no possibility of either fighting or fleeing, our tensed-up bodies have no opportunity of discharging the tension. People with fear of flying can therefore suffer from all sorts of distressing symptoms before, during, or after a flight, such as sleep problems, feeling hot or cold, sweating, headaches, dry mouth, stomach complaints, trembling, and muscle and joint pain. Because no action can be taken, we only experience the negative, uncomfortable physical sensations and emotions triggered by the fear.

In short, it is good and healthy for us to react with a certain degree of fear and tension in certain situations and in certain events. If we have a tendency to react with more fear than is appropriate in such situations, then the rule is: learn to control the fear, limit it, and tolerate a certain amount of anxiety and tension. And when the fear is triggered by situations or events that do not pose any objective danger, the rule is: learn to confront the situation, and in this way then to banish the fear.

As explained above, worrying about your fear reactions causes greater fear. When you misinterpret the physical feelings of fear, it becomes even more frightening. Unfortunately, a lot of people have the inaccurate belief that the physical feelings can lead to catastrophic outcomes, for example; 'losing control', 'going crazy', 'dying through suffering a heart attack' or 'fainting'. These beliefs will ensnare you into the circle described below. And as mentioned, these very ideas exacerbate your feelings of fear, which in turn increases your physical fear reactions, and further increases the fear itself (Figure 1).

It is important to overcome these misinterpretations. The physical reactions of fear are totally normal, as natural as bleeding when you cut yourself, or feeling pain

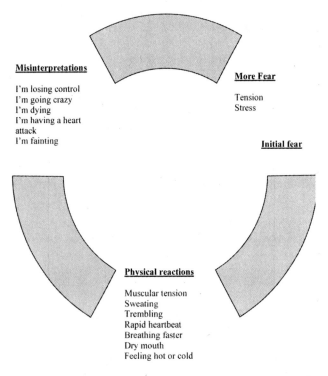

Misinterpretations

I'm losing control
I'm going crazy
I'm dying
I'm having a heart attack
I'm fainting

More Fear

Tension
Stress

Initial fear

Physical reactions

Muscular tension
Sweating
Trembling
Rapid heartbeat
Breathing faster
Dry mouth
Feeling hot or cold

Figure 1.

when you step on something sharp. The worst consequence of the fear is that it can make you very tired! If you are anxious, even a normal day can feel long, tiring, and perhaps difficult to get through. When you learn to deal with your fear, you get your energy back.

Do not give up on trying to deal with your fear – avoiding situations never gives you the chance to find out what the fear really is all about. Our advice is to carry on learning how to deal with your fear. Stop avoiding and find out what anxiety really is, it will enable you to step off the big spinning wheel shown in Figure 1.

The low down on the high up

Knowledge is power

Most people who are afraid of flying actually do things that maintain or even aggravate their fear, often without their being aware of this. One example is that they avoid good information about flying and aviation. When they do pay attention to information that concerns flying, it is usually in a form that 'justifies' or helps to maintain their fear, such as reading about air disasters or near misses. The person may point out to family and friends an aircraft accident somewhere in the world, and use this as a justification for why they themselves should avoid flying. It is really not so surprising that people who are afraid of flying tend to avoid all realistic information about the subject; after all, it is not just flying itself but all sorts of things connected with it that triggers their fear, and therefore it is no wonder that it is all to be avoided, wherever possible. Not paying attention to flying, aircraft, and related matters is part of this. This is a pity, as the word 'information' itself implies something that 'in-forms' or gives form to our thoughts and imagination. Incorrect or biased information, or a total lack of it, distorts our thoughts, so that we run the risk of thinking things that are wrong, or even bad for our well-being. Accordingly, this section will provide you with information about flying and everything connected with it.

You have made the choice to conquer your fear and one of the strategies in this fight, as you will see, is the fact that 'knowledge is power'.

We will provide knowledge about:

- International Civil Aviation Organization (ICAO);
- aerodynamics: what makes aircraft fly;
- aircraft and maintenance;
- cockpit crew;
- the cabin crew;
- air traffic control;
- the ticket;
- the airport;
- the flight itself;
- what is turbulence, and what causes it?;
- jet lag.

We will supply you with in-depth information about these subjects, and this knowledge can then give you the power to combat your fears. Read this section attentively, if necessary several times over, because, just as our thinking affects our feelings and behaviour, poor information can mean that we feel worse than we would with accurate information, and then we tend to behave inappropriately. Conversely, good information helps to bring our thinking, and thus our feeling and behaviour, back into line. Good information therefore does you good!

* * *

International Civil Aviation Organization (ICAO)

Even experienced air travellers seldom have much idea of all that is done before and during a flight in order to ensure its safety. Actually, this is not that surprising, since these activities are mostly carried out behind the scenes. Nothing is left to chance: there are regulations to cover everything. These regulations apply internationally, under the authority of the ICAO.

The aims of the ICAO are:

- to ensure that civil aviation proceeds in a safe and orderly way all over the world;
- to promote the safety of aircraft and flying;
- to lay down international standards for air traffic safety (i.e., safety criteria that have to be observed all over the world), and to promote ground aids.

All the rules described in the next sections are based on ICAO regulations.

Aerodynamics: what makes a plane fly?

There is no difference in principle between the way in which a large aircraft and a small aircraft fly; both make use of the same natural phenomena. Even paper aeroplanes and gliders obey these same laws of physics. Flying is based on the properties of air. Air is a substance: it has weight, and it has a certain density. Air is everywhere, so there is never any risk of an aircraft falling into a vacuum.

In order to get an aircraft into the air and keep it there, two forces have to be overcome: gravity and air resistance. Two forces are necessary for this: thrust, in the form of speed, and lift.

Originally, propellers were used to provide thrust for aircraft. A propeller (or 'airscrew' as pilots call it) is shaped so that it pushes the air back, which in turn propels the aircraft forward. In fact, it works in exactly the same way as a ship's propeller, which pushes back the water and so drives the ship forward.

The operation of a jet engine can best be compared with the action of a blown-up balloon when the air rushes out of the neck. The balloon forces the air through the opening, and is itself pushed in the opposite direction. A jet engine sucks in air, compresses it, mixes it with fuel and burns it, so building up a great pressure. As a result, the air emerges from the engine at a speed far greater than that at which it is sucked in. The engine (and with it the aircraft) is pushed forward in reaction. In addition to propeller engines and jet engines there is a third type, the turboprop engine, which is actually a combination of the first two.

A jet engine has many advantages over a propeller engine, in that it is:

- simpler and more powerful;
- made up of fewer moving parts;
- less subject to wear;
- easier to maintain;
- perhaps most importantly, safer and more reliable.

When a plane flies, the lift is provided by the wings, which have a special shape. The wing of an aircraft is flat underneath and curved outwards on top. When the engines give the aircraft speed, air flows over the wings (Figure 2).

The air travelling over the top of the wing has to travel a longer distance than the air travelling across the bottom. As a result, the air flowing over the top travels faster, in order to cover the greater distance in the same time, causing a lower pressure above the wing than below it. This lower pressure pulls or, as it were, sucks the aircraft upwards. The same natural phenomenon can be easily demonstrated at home by blowing across the top surface of a piece of paper: the paper is pulled upwards by the air flowing over the top. The lift of a plane depends on the shape of the wings and the speed at which the air flows over them. An easy way to understand this is to imagine the air above the wing being sucked into the smaller end of a funnel, as the funnel moves through the air. When the air leaves the funnel, the size of the funnel is larger, so therefore there is less density of air,

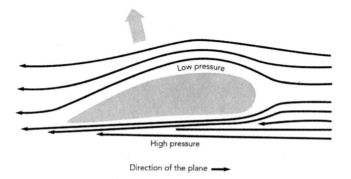

Figure 2. Wing profile.

37

occupying a larger space, and so the air pressure is lower (Figure 3).

Lift is also provided under the wings, due to their special downward angle. The air travelling under the wing has to travel a shorter distance than the air travelling over the top. As a result, the air flowing under the wing travels slower and is compressed, causing a higher pressure under the wing. This higher pressure works as a mattress or an airbed on which the aircraft is lying and pushing it upwards. This is also a natural phenomenon and can also be easily demonstrated at home by blowing into a balloon. There is higher pressure in the balloon, and when you let the air out of the balloon, and direct it to flow under a piece of paper which is lying flat, the paper is pushed upwards by the air flowing out of the balloon. Once again, imagine a funnel being moved through the air. This time, the air comes into the larger opening of the funnel, and leaves via the smaller opening. Because the same amount of air has to be compressed to pass through the smaller opening, the pressure is therefore higher when the air comes out of the funnel (Figure 4).

An aircraft moves in three dimensions. From the cockpit the pilots can move parts of the tail, main wings, and tail wings. To fly up or down, the elevator is used; this is a moveable part of the tail wing, mounted on the rear of the horizontal tail plane, that can swivel up or down. The

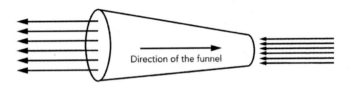

Direction of the funnel

Figure 3.   Funnel showing changes in air pressure above the wing.

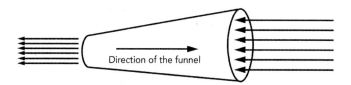

Direction of the funnel

Figure 4.   Funnel showing changes in air pressure below the wing.

rudder is mounted on the horizontal tail plane, and steers
the aircraft right or left. The ailerons are moveable parts
mounted on the edges of the wings, and are used to make
the aircraft bank to one side; they work inversely – when
one is going up the other one will go down. They are used
in conjunction with the rudder to make the aircraft turn
right or left. To illustrate why this is necessary, just think
of a motorcyclist, who not only has to steer by turning the
handlebars, but also has to lean to one side, or bank, in
order to corner.

The control movements, the lift and the thrust of an
aircraft are independent of each other. The moveable parts
of the wings (rudder, elevator, and ailerons) provide the
control, the wings the lift, and the engines the thrust. This
means that even in the statistically highly unlikely case of
all engines of a multi-engine aircraft failing at once, the
aircraft does not 'fall out of the sky' but continues to glide
forward and remains under control. If the engines are all
stopped at once when the aircraft is at cruising height, it
can easily continue to glide for between 150 to 200 miles.
In other words, the pilots have plenty of time and space
to find a safe landing place. In fact, during a normal
descent the engines do not provide any thrust; they are
allowed to idle, and the aircraft glides downwards. Think
of what happens when you take your foot off the acceler-
ator of your car, and disengage the clutch – the car slowly

rolls along until it gently stops. Or an even better example: think of what happens when you are going down a long steep hill on your bicycle.

The possibility of all engines of a multi-engine craft failing at once is extremely remote. The chance of two modern jet engines failing during a flight will be around one in 1,000,000,000 flying hours. Even if half the engines fail, the aircraft is still able to gain height, even if this happens immediately after take-off. An aircraft flying without the use of one of its engines can still easily reach its destination. However, when an aircraft has an engine failure soon after take-off, most of the time it will simply return immediately to the same airport, rather than continue with the flight.

People sometimes think – wrongly – that lightning can cause engine failure. Nothing could be further from the truth. Passengers in an aircraft need not be afraid of lightning. An aircraft that is struck by lightening does not suffer any adverse effects: the craft acts as a 'Faraday cage', so that the voltage remains on the outside and leaks away into the air. If the aircraft is sitting on the ground, conductive material in the tyres leads the voltage away to earth. In either case, the people inside the aircraft are not affected in any way.

Aircraft and maintenance

Aircraft designers and builders devote a great deal of time (years, in fact), not to mention a great deal of money, on testing new planes.

An aircraft has to be not only safe and reliable, but also stable. This stability means that, if left to its own devices, the aircraft will never go into a roll or a turn by itself. The material of which the craft is built has to be strong, but must also offer certain flexibility, because air is always in motion. Thanks to the flexibility of the wings, no problem is caused by turbulence or eddies in the air. Further, the material must be able to resist large differences in temperature. If, for example, the aircraft takes off in a hot country and climbs to cruising height, the temperature can go from + 40° to −60° Celsius. All these factors have to be taken into account when designing an aircraft.

After the prototype is built, one or two years are normally spent testing the aircraft. Not until the manufacturer is convinced that the product is satisfactory in every way is it submitted to the aviation authority for approval. The machine is then inspected and tested once more by all the aviation authorities of all the countries in which the aircraft will become registered. Only when the airline is satisfied of its airworthiness is the aircraft awarded a type certificate. The body responsible for issuing the certificate is the ICAO (International Civil Aviation Organization), and after this, there is the CAA (Civil Aviation Authority) in the UK, and in the USA the FAA (Federal Aviation Authority). In addition to the type certificate, each individual aircraft of the particular type has to receive its own airworthiness certificate from the aviation authority of the country in which it will based. Since the latter certificate is only valid for a certain length of time, the aircraft has to undergo full inspection at regular intervals in order to have its certificate renewed.

This means that before you board a plane it has been awarded its certification according to the standards of:

1. the building factory;
2. the ICAO;

3. the national aviation authority of the country in which the aircraft is built;
4. The national aviation authority of the countries in which the aircraft will fly;
5. The airline or company itself.

For example, if British Airways bought a Boeing 777 from the Boeing Company in the USA, the following certificates would be required:

1. a certificate from Boeing itself;
2. the ICAO certificate;
3. a certificate from the FAA of the USA;
4. the CAA in the UK;
5. British Airways itself.

The owner of the aircraft is also obliged to observe the regulations for maintenance, repair, and overhaul of the aircraft. The term 'maintenance' covers all the periodic activities necessary to keep the aircraft in good, airworthy condition. Only qualified experts – specially trained engineers, can carry out maintenance. The national aviation authority, for its part, checks that maintenance is carried out correctly and at the required times.

Each aircraft has a particular maintenance schedule, which is used to check whether maintenance is carried out at the correct times. There are five types of maintenance, indicated by letters of the alphabet, which are used by most airlines. After every flight, the ground engineers carry out an inspection. In addition, the flight recorder (commonly known as the 'black box', although in actual fact it is coloured orange–pink) and the air data recorder record everything that happens to the aircraft. For example, a too-hard landing is automatically recorded; the captain can never cover up such an incident, and every irregularity in the flight will always be investigated. Nowadays there are computers on board that regularly carry out checks and automatically send reports to the airport about the technical status of the aircraft (Aircraft Communications and Reporting System, ACARS). If anything is not as it should be, the aircraft goes to the hangar for what we call B maintenance. The C maintenance is much more extensive and is carried out after each 300–350 hours of flying, depending on the type of aircraft. The D maintenance is performed every 11–12 months, and involves a comprehensive inspection. After four or five years comes the biggest maintenance task of all, the E maintenance. For instance, for a Boeing 747 this means that this inspection will be performed after five years or 26,000 flying hours, whichever comes first.

The work involved in the E maintenance takes about two to three months. The entire aircraft is taken apart; every nut and bolt is carefully checked and, if necessary, replaced. Virtually the entire aircraft is checked for metal fatigue, micro-cracking, and corrosion. The inspection techniques used include X-ray and gamma ray inspection. Afterwards, the aircraft is in excellent technical condition, arguably as good as new. Many components such as engines, landing gear, and instruments have their own additional maintenance schedule, taken care of for every aircraft by the technical department. Here it is worth noting that pilots never depend on a single instrument; there are two, three, or in some cases even more of each instrument on board.

While in this information section we have looked at many aspects of air safety, we are still very far from

43

covering all the relevant measures and regulations – that would take too much time and space. However, what we have covered makes clear the extraordinary lengths that are gone to in order to maximize the safety of air travel.

Cockpit crew

Sometimes there are more than just pilots in the cockpit. In older types of aircraft there is also a flight engineer. All members of the cockpit crew have very extensive training. It takes many years before somebody can, for instance, become a captain of a Boeing 747. A UK airline pilot usually begins his or her flying training at a flying school. A great number of people apply to these institutions every year, but only the very best manage to pass the strict selection procedures – out of every 100 people applying, only two are accepted. The selection process includes a thorough medical examination and psychological testing, plus examination of aptitude and motivation.

The training at a flying school lasts approximately two years, with trainees living in most of the time. The future pilots learn to fly various types of aircraft. They begin with small, simple, single-engine propeller craft, and graduate by stages to complex, multi-engine jets. Usually after two years they obtain the highest level of pilot's licence, an ATPL (Airline Transport Pilot Licence), with so-called twin rating and IFR (Instrument Flying Rating) certificate. However, the certificate of competence does not allow the pilot to fly any type of aircraft, but only the specific model for which the test has been completed. For each type of aircraft there is a different exam. In this respect the certificate of competence differs from a driver's licence, which enables the holder to drive any kind of car. To obtain their certificate of competence, pilots not only have to pass tests but also have to pass a medical examination and clock up a specified large number of hours of experience. This experience is recorded in a logbook, which every pilot must keep. It is used to keep a record of the flying time, with the date, the number of hours and minutes flown, the tasks carried out in the cockpit, and the type of aircraft.

Graduates from the aviation school can call themselves pilots, but that is far from being the end of the story. To start with, the certificate of competence is only valid for one year. After that, pilots have to undergo another medical examination, and must have flown a sufficient number of hours during the year to keep their experience up to the required standard. They then have to pass further practical tests in order to show that they are still competent to fly. If everything is as it should be, then the certificate of competence is extended for another year, but if just one part of the test is unsatisfactory, then the pilot is grounded until the whole test has been successfully completed. Pilots also have to make at least three take-offs and landings in 'their' type of aircraft every three months. If they do not, then they have to follow further courses before they are allowed to fly again.

Those who graduate from the aviation school can apply to join the flying staff of an airline. If they are accepted, they go straight back to school to be trained on the type of craft flown by the company concerned. Airline pilots always fly on only one type of aircraft. The newly employed pilots start a theoretical training about the aircraft they are going to fly in order to become perfectly familiar with all the aspects of that aircraft. Once they have mastered the theory, they learn to fly the aircraft on a flight simulator.

The flight simulator is a mock-up of a cockpit, supported on pistons that can tilt it in various directions. Every possible situation that can occur during a flight can be simulated, with the instructor playing 'Fate' through the intermediary of a computer. For example, the instructor can make any or all of the engines fail, or change the weather conditions. In this way, the pilot learns to handle such situations, should they ever occur in real life. During landings and take-offs, the pilot, looking through the window of the make-believe cockpit, sees a realistic image of a runway projected on a screen. The simulator can be programmed to show the actual runway at airports all over the world. Pilots practising in a flight simulator often forget that in fact they are sitting safely on the ground, so realistic is the effect. When making a hard landing or flying through turbulence, the pilot actually feels the bumps!

Each flight in a simulator is performed with the full cockpit crew present, plus an instructor. And, since the simulator reacts just like a real aircraft, exams are taken in it. The simulator training ends with a simulated flight during which both theory and practice are tested. The flight, for instance, from Heathrow to Amsterdam, lasts as long as it would in reality, and the pilot has to carry out the same operations as in an actual flight.

If all goes well, the pilot continues the training in a real aircraft. He or she then flies by him/herself, but still under the supervision of an instructor who sits beside him or her and watches carefully everything that is done. The instructor in this case is a captain who at other times flies normal flights, but who also has training duties. After a set number of hours of flying, the trainee pilot takes yet another test. An experienced pilot then takes over from

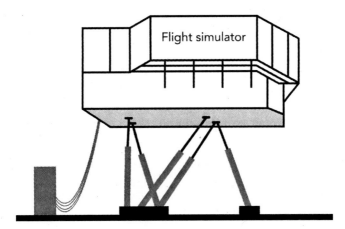

Figure 5. Flight simulator.

the instructor and begins the route training on normal passenger flights. In this way, the new pilot learns all about the route to be flown. In the meantime, the instructor sits behind the two pilots, but is now acting simply as an observer, or "safety pilot". This continues for several more trips, until the "apprentice" can fly just as well as the captain.

Meanwhile, the pilot follows a ground-based course of knowledge about routes and airports. The pilot learns everything about the route to a particular destination: discrete features of the landscape; the weather in the regions to be overflown; the approach paths; the layout of the airport and its runways; and alternative airports at which it is also possible to land. The training is carried out with the help of films, slides, and written reports. The training for a particular type of aircraft is the same for both co-pilot and captain; both must be able to do everything on their own. Once the pilot has completed training, he or she starts to work as a co-pilot. Promotion to captain follows only after a great deal of experience. The captain determines the division of tasks during the flight. Usually, captain and co-pilot take it in turn to do things. For example, the co-pilot might fly and navigate from Birmingham to Tenerife while the captain maintains radio contact; for the return trip they switch jobs, so that both keep their skills up to scratch.

Even once a pilot is fully trained, the certificate of competence is still only valid for a year. Every year there is a new medical check-up, with strict standards to be achieved. Also every year there is a proficiency test, known informally as the "prof check", demanded by the ICAO and the Civil Aviation Authority. The prof check is usually done in the flight simulator. If the pilot does not pass, further training follows until the required level to take a further exam is achieved. If that is failed, then there is the prospect of dismissal. Between prof checks there are upgrading courses in the simulator, with new procedures and techniques being demonstrated and practised.

In very few other professions do people have to demonstrate their competence as often as in civil aviation. A pilot has to keep studying throughout his/her professional life, and continually faces the risk of dismissal due to under-performance or physical defects. Every flight is in fact a test, in a very real way; if a co-pilot under-performs, the captain is obliged to report this to the superior. Conversely, a co-pilot is also expected to report under-performance on the part of the captain.

Flight engineers

Flight engineers are trained at a technical college or technical university, and receive further training from the airline. A flight engineer is a highly-trained expert in aircraft technology. Just as the pilot is only licensed to fly one type of aircraft, so the flight engineer only deals with a single type of plane, which he or she knows literally inside out, from engine to air-conditioning, including every wire or pipe of every system, whether electrical, hydraulic, or mechanical. The profession is actually dying out, since the skills of the flight engineer are mostly superfluous on the modern generation of aircraft. All the information that pilots used to obtain from the flight engineer, because they themselves could not monitor certain engine instruments, is now provided by computer screens in front of them. Flight engineers are now employed only on the old DC 10 and the older Boeing 747–200, 747–300 and 727 aircraft.

Cockpit crew at work

The work of the pilots and, if there is one, the flight engineer, begins about an hour and a half before the flight. They report to their airline's duty desk at the airport, where they are given information about the load, the fuel, the flight plan, and other relevant information about the aircraft. They then carry out a careful check of every part of the aircraft on the basis of checklists. Everything is covered: the landing gear, the tyres, the wing surfaces, the flaps, the rudders, and the skin of the aircraft. They make sure that the tanks have been filled with the right amount of fuel. The quantity must be more than enough to reach an alternative airport, after arriving at their destination, should this be necessary for any reason. Even if the plane flies to its original destination and then to an alternative airport, there still has to be a comfortable reserve of fuel.

Only once everything has been found correct do they take over responsibility for the plane from the technical services; from that moment, the aircraft is declared to be technically airworthy.

The pilots then go through the flight plan. This is a standard form drawn up by the ICAO on which the route and all flight details have to be entered. The airline has to file the flight plan well in advance with the Flight Information Office (FIO). The FIO forwards it by data link to the air traffic control centres of all areas that the aircraft will cross on its flight. Once they have run through the flight plan, the pilots go to the air travel meteorological department, i.e., the weather department, which informs them about the weather at the present time, the forecast of the weather conditions along the route, plus the options for alternative routes and alternative airports. The pilots next go to the Flight Information Office, where they obtain information about any possible changes in the frequencies of radio beacons and transmitters, and about the radar installation of the air traffic control centres with which they will be dealing. They also obtain last-minute information about the departure and arrival airports. The flight plan is processed in the Flight Information Office. It is now time for the pilots to enter the cockpit, where they enter all the information of the routing into the flight computers and, after that, run through the standard checklists. These are 'say and do' checklists: the first person reads out the items one by one, the other carries out the check and answers in the prescribed way so that there can be no misunderstandings. The entire operation of the aircraft is checked in this way, making sure, among other things, that all the instruments work correctly and all the switches are in the proper position.

Before the engines are started up, the cockpit crew listens to a recording of the latest information on the weather and specific information of the airport itself. The pilot then requests permission from the control tower for the aircraft to be pushed back, if this is necessary, and for the engines to be started. The point of this is to avoid leaving the engines running too long – thus wasting fuel – if there is a delay. The engines are started up according to a set procedure, with the pilots and the flight engineer (if there is one) working as a team. The crew carefully checks every aspect and this checking continues throughout the flight. Once the engines have been started, the pilot requests permission from the control tower to taxi to the take-off runway. While taxiing, the crew runs through yet another checklist. The air traffic control centre gives them route clearance, meaning that the complete route has been definitively set and is clear all along the way. The pilots instruct the cabin personnel – the flight attendants – to prepare for take-off, and then ask the control tower for permission to take off. The take-off is done by one of the pilots, while the other continually checks that everything is in order. The division of tasks between the captain and co-pilot during the flight has already been predetermined.

Once the aircraft has reached cruising height, things become somewhat less busy for the pilots, although they continue to monitor their instruments at all times and keep two-way radio contact with air traffic control. Since the aircraft is now being flown by the automatic pilot, the workload is lower and one pilot can easily deal with everything. Once the descent commences, everybody becomes busy once more. The descent sometimes begins more than 150 miles from the airport. The landing is a standard procedure, just like the take-off.

Once the plane has arrived at the airport, the pilots note all the particulars of the flight in the logbooks. If the flight has been a long one, they then have to take an obligatory rest period. The ICAO imposes a strict schedule of work and rest, and the Civil Aviation Authority makes sure that it is observed. Cockpit crew members fly on average between 600 and a maximum 1,000 hours per year. Their job, of course, is more than flying; it also includes the flight preparation time and the time spent waiting at airports. Just compare this with people in other responsible jobs, who often work more than forty hours per week for at least forty-five weeks per year, i.e., more than 1,800 hours per year. By imposing a maximum of 1,000 flying hours per year, the Civil Aviation Authority ensures that pilots remain fit for their job.

The cabin crew

The cabin personnel consist mostly of a purser, sometimes with an assistant purser, plus the flight attendants. Their main tasks are to ensure safety and to care for the passengers, under the authority of the purser. The cabin crew are trained by the airline. In this case the training is valid for a maximum number of only three aircraft. One of the most important courses is flight safety. This course has to be retaken at regular intervals, and cabin personnel have to take an annual test. It covers all general safety measures, together with particular safety measures for the types of aircraft covered by the training. The cabin personnel have to know all the tasks so thoroughly that they can carry them out automatically, in the shortest possible time. This is important for such events as evacuating the passengers from the aircraft as quickly as possible in case of an emergency. The requirement that the ICAO and the Civil

Aviation Authority have laid down is that it must be possible to get all the passengers out of the aircraft within ninety seconds (yes, one and a half minutes!), even if half the doors and emergency exits are blocked.

In addition to flight safety, cabin personnel are also trained in first aid. The purser is trained to a still higher level, so that he or she not only knows what to do in case of such incidents as a heart attack, but can even deliver a baby. The most important thing to remember, however, is that the cabin crew know what to do in an emergency. The initial training takes about five weeks, and, as has been mentioned, their performance is regularly checked and their training updated.

One and a half hours before the flight, the cabin personnel meet to arrange the division of tasks on board and to discuss any special arrangements for the flight: for example, if there are passengers with medical conditions, or requiring special assistance. A check is carried out before the flight to make sure everything necessary is on board. For example, the stocks of food in the pantry must be complete. There not only has to be the correct number of ordinary meals, but also any special meals which have been ordered such as low fat, low salt, sugar-free, or vegetarian. The check covers huge lists of things: are there nappies for babies, newspapers in various languages, tax-free articles, and, if required, wheelchairs and crutches?

The purser and crew welcome the passengers on board and direct them to their seats. Before take-off, the cabin crew check that everybody has fastened their safety belt, the seats are upright and the tables are folded away. While the plane is taxiing, the cabin personnel point out the information in the pocket on the back of the seat facing each passenger. They show where the emergency exits are, and demonstrate how to use the oxygen masks and life jackets. All this is carried out according to prescribed safety procedures. While the plane is taking off and landing, the crew members sit beside the doors and emergency exits. During the flight they serve drinks and meals, the latter being warmed in special ovens. One of the flight attendants also serves the cockpit crew with food and drink. The captain and co-pilot are served different meals, and do not eat at the same time. As you can see, nothing is left to chance – even the risk of both pilots getting food poisoning is eliminated.

Air traffic control

The task of air traffic control is to direct aircraft along their routes all over the world, and to ensure that they do not come too close to one another. Air traffic control also makes it possible for aircraft to fly in cloud, without sight of the ground.

Each country in principle has its own air traffic control, and the different control centres are all in contact with each other. They all follow rules laid down by the ICAO: for instance, concerning the distance that has to be maintained between aircraft. Another rule is that all communication must be in English. The time used for air traffic all over the world is UTC (Universal Time Co-ordinated), the former Greenwich Mean Time. This means that a pilot who wishes to land in Hong Kong speaks English, is answered by air traffic control in the same language, and has the same time on his clock as a pilot flying over Gatwick at that moment.

The international airports are linked by 'airways', imaginary corridors through the air with a width of ten miles and a prescribed floor and ceiling height. At a large airport, the airways terminate in an 'air traffic area', a large, circular area that in turn connects with an imaginary cylinder extending upwards from the ground. Within this cylinder there are separate routes for approaching and departing traffic (Figure 6).

The air traffic control is made up of different teams, each with responsibility for part of the overall route. The control tower commences guiding the aircraft on its route when the pilot asks permission to start up the engines and begin taxiing. At this point, all the air traffic control teams have already checked that the route is clear; if it is not, permission to start the engines is not given. The pilot is given precise instructions on where to turn right or left when taxiing, and where to stop and wait. The local controller in the tower then takes over, telling the pilot when clearance has been given for take-off, and guiding the pilot to a height of 3,000 feet. The approach and

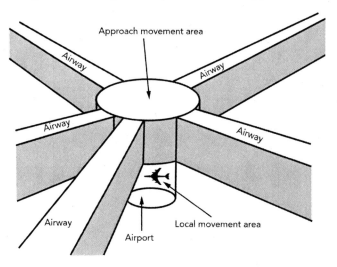

Figure 6. Air traffic control chart.

departure controller next brings the aircraft on to its route. He or she is assisted by computers and radar guidance systems. The controller watches a computer display with the altitude and position of each aircraft. The display also shows the type of plane, its call sign, its speed, relevant information about the route being flown, the airport of origin, and the airport of destination. In this way, the controller can check whether the pilot is following instructions correctly.

Civil airliners have weather radar in the cockpit, giving the pilots advance warning of the weather and enabling them to modify the route in order to avoid storms. However, any changes to the route must, of course, be communicated to, and approved by, air traffic control.

The pilot knows the position of the aircraft at each moment. The airways are 'signposted' by radio beacons, each with its own recognition code. Closer to an airport, the number of beacons tends to increase. Some of these beacons are used by aircraft in order to fly a holding pattern whenever the airport is too busy for the plane to land at a particular moment. The decision to send an aircraft into a holding pattern is taken by air traffic control. The holding pattern consists of a 'stack' of aircraft circling at different heights, and is located at a safe distance away from the airport. Whenever a landing slot becomes free, the lowest aircraft is fetched from the stack. Each aircraft is then instructed, one at a time, to descend to the next lowest level of the stack, and confirmation of this received before the following aircraft is instructed to move down a level.

During the runway approach, the radio beacons and air traffic control keep the pilot on the correct course (horizontal) and angle of descent (vertical) at each moment.

The pilot sees this information on the cockpit instruments, while the control tower follows the aircraft on the radar screen. The information provided by these systems is so accurate that the pilot is able to approach the runway even in weather conditions that would make ordinary driving impossible.

The air traffic controllers in the tower and in front of the radar screens never work more than two hours per shift, after which they take a half-hour break. Trainee and assistant air traffic controllers go through a strict selection procedure, and by the time they become fully qualified air traffic controllers they already have many years of experience. They begin at the bottom, and for each promotion they must have sufficient experience and pass an examination. If they do not pass the exam, they do not have any further prospects of promotion.

Distance between planes

To protect planes from colliding in the air, the TCAS system has been developed. TCAS stands for Traffic Collision and Avoidance System and works on the basis of interrogation of planes in the surrounding area, by means of the transponder. TCAS therefore scans the vicinity by interrogating the transponders of other aircraft. It then uses the received transponder signals to compute distance, bearing, and altitude relative to its own aircraft. Thus, using the answers to the interrogation given by the plane, the relative position of other planes is specified. Changes of position are then used to provide warning of potential collision. Figure 7 depicts areas that reflect a certain level of warning. In the caution volume, the approaching traffic is coloured yellow. The pilot is thus warned that

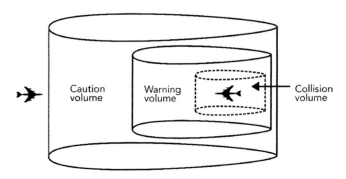

Figure 7. Traffic Collision and Avoidance System: TCAS.

another plane might come too close. The time for the other plane to penetrate the collision volume is then still 40–45 seconds. In the warning volume, the approaching traffic is marked red and the transponders of both planes will co-ordinate a solution. Remaining time until entering the collision volume is still twenty-five seconds. The transponders ensure then that one plane will climb while the other plane will descend.

Turbulence

Research has shown that, more than any other aspect of flying, turbulence causes fear among passengers. The main question, of course, is, is it dangerous or merely uncomfortable? In this section we would like to answer that question and look at turbulence in detail, in order to clear up any possible misunderstandings. Such misconceptions tend to arise because turbulence is a favourite topic of tall tales designed to impress other people with assertions such as 'the aircraft suddenly plunged 6,000 feet' or 'we hit a gigantic air pocket'. Unfortunately, such tales are sometimes picked up the by the media and misrepresented as really dangerous situations. An accurate report, being fully informed, would have said that there was no danger involved. Turbulence is not a safety issue. It is a comfort issue.

Misinformation about turbulence can be very frightening. Imagine that tomorrow you have to take a trip. Before you went to bed, a friend told you about his most recent flight, in which he experienced serious turbulence. That night, after sleeping for a while, you find yourself wide awake. Thoughts of the following day flood your mind – that trip by air, which you have put off as long as possible, but which you at last have to take in the morning. What will happen if you also experience that turbulence? The longer you dwell on the thoughts, the wider awake you become. And the more determined you are that 'I really must get back to sleep soon, because if I don't get a good night's sleep, I won't be fit tomorrow', the less likely you are to fall asleep. The result of these worrying thoughts – both of the turbulence, and of the urgent need to sleep – is that you really do begin to feel threatened and as if you are in danger. Your body starts to respond, with your muscles becoming taut, your breathing speeding up, and you start to toss and turn restlessly in the bed. We continually run the risk of experiencing fear due solely to a danger summoned up by our imagination, without being fully aware of the facts.

This phenomenon plays an important role in the fear of turbulence, because many people with a fear of flying are also afraid of turbulence. During a flight in an area with moderate to severe turbulence, the body's alarm bells start to ring wildly, and the danger signals start to flash. For those people, turbulence equals danger! The association is clear, and so fear arises. People who are afraid of turbulence sometimes develop a double fear: fear of what could happen to the aircraft when flying through turbulence, and fear of what could happen to their body if they become anxious during turbulence. The point is that both fears are the product of a perceived threat, but it is one which does not have an external validity.

As we have emphasized, turbulence is not a question of safety, but of comfort. When there is turbulence in the air, you get shaken about a bit, it is more difficult to read, or to eat and drink without making a mess. You have to fasten your safety belt, and you cannot go to the toilet. This is simply to prevent passengers getting hurt by banging into something as a result of the shaking. For these reasons, turbulence can be inconvenient or uncomfortable, but it is not dangerous – it does not pose any threat to the safety of the aircraft. For this purpose it helps to have a good understanding of exactly what turbulence is, and so we will look at this in detail.

Pilots define turbulence in terms of its degree: light, moderate, or severe. In light turbulence, you may feel your seatbelt occasionally pressing against you as the aircraft gently shakes and rocks. In moderate turbulence, the shaking is stronger and more uneven; now and then you feel yourself being pressed into your seat or against your safety belt, and the tea in your cup will start to slop. Loose objects may start to move, in the same way as a small box will move across the dashboard of your car when you turn into a bend. Objects lying loose on the floor may start to jump about, as happens when you drive too quickly over a speed bump in the road. Severe turbulence occurs only infrequently, and usually does not last very long (a few minutes at most). Turbulence can generally be predicted, but not always, especially as light turbulence can occur spontaneously. On most flights you are allowed to undo your safety belt, but it may happen that there is light to moderate turbulence during the whole flight, in which case it is better to keep your safety belt on.

To reiterate, turbulence is simply the shaking of the aircraft caused by air in motion. It is not caused by air pockets – in fact, there is no such thing as a vacuum or a pocket without air anywhere in the atmosphere. 'Air pockets' do not exist at all!

It is useful to remember the following facts.

Air is not 'nothing'. Air is 'something'; it is matter, and consists of particles. Air is a gas, and just like in any gas, the particles move in the same way as in a fluid. Air moves along in waves, just as water does. When two different currents – and thus two different wave motions – meet each other, the movement of the water is disturbed, causing jerky movements of the boat. The same phenomenon occurs when two layers of air with different speeds and wave motions travel past each other. In our atmosphere, we regularly have two layers of air moving past each other. As we go higher, the wind becomes stronger and changes in direction.

If you travel by boat on a calm day, there are no waves and you will have a smooth trip. In windy weather, there are waves on the water and the trip is rougher. The comparison largely holds true for air travel. In fact, an aircraft flying through the air moves in a similar fashion to a fish swimming through water. It is important to understand that warm air is lighter and rises, while cold air falls because it is denser, in the same way as happens with water of different temperatures. This rise and fall of the warm and cold air causes vertical movements in our atmosphere, and naturally the aircraft reacts to these. The temperature inside a cloud is generally lower than in the surrounding air. The differences in temperature lead to an exchange of energy, thus causing motion.

There are many other types of meteorological activity that can influence the movement of aircraft, but for the aircraft itself they are unimportant; the aircraft sits in the middle of a whole mass of air, moving along with it in the same way as a fish swims along within the current, which is within the whole mass of water in which it moves.

Turbulence cannot harm an aircraft or any part of it, neither the fuselage, nor the wings, nor the skin. Aircraft are designed to withstand 2.5 times the strongest turbulence ever observed. It can be uncomfortable for the people inside the aircraft, as loose objects can fall and cause damage. But when we ourselves are fastened into our seat, we are in fact attached to the skin of the aircraft, and nothing can happen to us. For pilots, turbulence, even moderate turbulence, is no more than a tolerable nuisance, although for the sake of comfort they do everything possible to avoid it. Inside the cabin, everything is fastened in position in order to prevent it falling, and the flight attendants also have to sit down and fasten their safety belts so as not to hurt themselves. If everything and everybody is strapped down, then turbulence is no more than an inconvenience. However, although pilots know that turbulence has nothing to do with safety, they also do not like to be shaken and therefore they do everything possible to avoid severe turbulence.

Our advice during a flight when you experience turbulence and feel nervous is, read this section again and do not skip the following 'mantra', but on the contrary read it attentively, if necessary several times, and say it out loud.

'TURBULENCE IS NOT A SAFETY ISSUE,
IT'S A COMFORT ISSUE!'

Repeat this sentence to yourself during turbulence as long as necessary!

Do not try to resist the shaking, as this means tensing your muscles unnecessarily; just ride with it, as you would on a horse, or in a train, bus, car, or on a motorbike, but make sure you wear your seat belt. If you learn to tell yourself during turbulence, 'This isn't dangerous, just inconvenient', then the level of anxiety will most probably decrease, and so will the false alarm symptoms experienced by your body.

The journey through your journey

In this chapter we give a description of everything that happens during a plane trip. For nervous flyers, some of the things can be worrying. This often has to do with the fact that they do not know what is happening, or why it is happening. Once they know what is going on, then the events tend to lose their threatening impression. Starting from the decision to fly, we cover everything that happens during the flight, right up to coming out of the airport at the 'other end'.

The ticket

Let us begin with the purchase of a ticket. It used to be the case that, if you were travelling by air, you had to buy your ticket from either the High Street travel agent or the airline. An airline ticket would be issued. This is more than just a card; it is a little book in itself. If you look at it you will see it is full of abbreviations. In addition to the flight times, the ticket contains the 'conditions of carriage', which in fact form a contract between the passenger and the airline. There are also rules and regulations about what to do if your luggage is damaged or gets lost.

While previously all tickets were purchased through airlines or travel agents, the Internet has widened the choice for many people, and as well as booking over the Internet with a travel agent, and receiving an airline ticket through the post, you can also book what is known as an 'e-ticket'. This gives a reference number, which, when presented at the airport, usually with the e-mail confirmation, and the payment card that you used for the transaction, shows the staff the details of your booking, and allows a boarding card to be issued.

The safety regulations for flying are much stricter than for any other means of transport. When you buy an air ticket, the travel agency usually asks if you want to take out travel insurance. 'Why should I need travel insurance,' the fledgling flyer may ask. The answer is that there are many situations in which insurance is useful – illness or an accident abroad, or the loss of one's luggage, passport, or money, all of which have nothing to do with the safety of air travel. Travel insurance for an air journey is no different from insurance for a trip by train, bus, and car, or any other means of transport, and is no more expensive. The primary difference is that when one is away from the UK, one no longer has access to such facilities as the National Health Service. The travel insurance can also provide cover in the unlikely event of financial problems with one's travel company; ensuring one is able to return more easily than would otherwise be the case.

There is now a European Health Insurance Card (EHIC), which entitles you to reduced-cost, sometimes free, medical treatment if that becomes necessary while you are in a European Economic Area (EEA) country or Switzerland. People are advised to obtain one before travelling abroad. The EHIC also covers any treatment you need for a chronic disease or pre-existing illness. You need to make arrangements in advance for kidney dialysis and oxygen therapy. To arrange for kidney dialysis while you are away, contact your NHS renal unit in the UK before you travel. For limited information on oxygen supply services in the EEA countries and Switzerland, call the Department of Health's Customer Service Centre on 020 7210 4850. Remember that the EHIC will not cover you if getting medical treatment is the main purpose of your trip. You are advised to take out comprehensive private insurance for visits to all countries, regardless of whether you are covered by your EHIC. Your EHIC should cover you for routine maternity care while you are away. However, if you are going to an EEA country or Switzerland specifically to have your baby, you will need an E112 form.

Many people wonder why there is a limit on the weight of luggage that can be taken on the flight. The reason is that for travel by air, the fuel costs depend on the weight. In actual fact, you are allowed to take more luggage than the maximum mentioned on the ticket, but you will have to pay extra for it. The cost for excess luggage tends to be high, so it can be worth keeping to one's allowance. You may want to pack less than your weight allowance to be able to bring back your holiday purchases!

Finally, you may ask yourself why the ticket specifies in such detail what may and may not be taken in the luggage and hand luggage. This is a precaution: an aircraft cabin is pressurized, and every care is taken to ensure that it remains so. Likewise, the rules about dangerous items are self explanatory, and are there as a safety measure for all passengers. Just remember that these rules are purely there for safety considerations.

First and Business Class

Flying in Business or First Class is more expensive than Economy. However, there are substantial advantages, not only for the flight itself, but also before and after it. The key differences include such facilities as checking in at special 'fast track' counters, and being permitted a greater luggage allowance. After checking in, there is often a 'fast track' route through security. You then have access to a special lounge area, in which food, beverages, reading material, as well as computer access, are normally freely available. Your ticket is normally flexible, and so if you inadvertently miss your flight, perhaps because you are delayed getting to the airport, or even just wish to change your plans, it is possible to re-book at no extra cost. The reduction in stress and additional comfort can be helpful.

Boarding is normally prioritized, so you can both get on and off the plane before the Economy passengers. Sitting towards the front of the plane, you hardly hear the engines, and any turbulence is far less noticeable. There is a greater choice of superior quality food and drink, and the service is considerably faster, as the ratio of crew to passengers is substantially higher. The difference is particularly evident when you fly inter-continentally in the larger planes.

Seats are normally wider in Business and First Class, with additional leg room, and often for longer flights they can be reclined into a flat or almost flat bed. The audio-visual choice of entertainment is considerably greater, and can be played 'on demand', whereas in Economy you frequently have to wait until all the films are finished, before they all run through a second and perhaps a third time. The extra space feels more comfortable. Your 'personal territory' is much larger, and you are therefore less likely to feel as if your 'personal space' is being violated, given the greater distance between passengers.

When you land, First and Business Class passengers are normally the first to be allowed off the plane. Your luggage frequently has a priority tagging, which means it is likely to be unloaded and available for collection from the carousel sooner than the luggage of other passengers. You are therefore able to leave the airport sooner than would otherwise be the case, after having cleared Customs in the normal way. As mentioned, however, all this comfort does come at a price.

The airport

If you are going on an international flight, you generally have to be at the airport two or three hours before departure. For flights within Europe you have to be there two hours early, while for domestic flights you are expected to check in an hour before the flight. These times can change, depending on levels of security, so make sure you check the advice each time you fly. Likewise, different airports and airlines specify different times, so it is always worth checking in advance. Running out of time will only increase your anxiety. Given the timings, this means you will be spending some time in the airport before you go on board.

The airport terminal is usually very busy – an international hubbub of strange impressions – and having to wait there can be trying for novice passengers. Even the public address system can be unsettling, when the polite but unearthly voice announces flights arriving from and departing to all parts of the world.

The sense of other-worldliness is heightened by the safety measures and the plethora of signs and directions: arrivals, departures, terminal, tax/duty-free, charter (an aircraft hired for a single flight, usually by a travel agency, as opposed to a regular flight to a particular destination), check-in (for ticket inspection, seat reservation, and weighing-in of luggage), gate (the exit that takes you to the aircraft). You, as a passenger, are forced into a dependent, passive position. You have to comply with the safety regulations, submit to the Customs and Immigration formalities, observe the waiting times, hand over your luggage and allow your bags to be searched. If you are normally assertive and independent, you may get tense and irritated because you can no longer do things the way you choose.

Having taken your luggage to the check-in desk, you will be asked for your ticket and passport, and asked a series of standard security questions. Even for domestic flights it is now necessary to produce photo-identification – your passport or a driving licence with your photo on it. The simplest solution is to always remember to take your passport. It is worth noting that some airlines allow you to pre-book a preferred seat over the Internet, so this is reserved for you when you check in. Following presentation of your ticket, or e-ticket reference, you will be given your boarding pass and assigned seat number, and told when your flight will be boarding, and from which gate. Self-service check-in desks are becoming increasingly common – a machine reads your passport and booking reference, and can even give you the option of choosing your preferred seat, as can the check-in staff. In the case of self-service, once the machine has issued your boarding pass, you take your luggage to the 'luggage drop-off' point, and leave it there.

You then usually have to queue to go through Security, where you and your hand luggage will be screened. There will normally be time for something (non alcoholic!) to drink, or a snack, or even some 'retail therapy' – the selection of shopping outlets can be quite impressive. If you are travelling internationally, you may be able to buy at duty-free prices, but be warned – duty-free is not profit-free! There are usually television screens that announce the flights, showing any delays, and telling you when to proceed to the numbered departure gate. In smaller airports this information tends to be given over the announcement system.

Your flight is called, and you proceed to the boarding gate, where there is often a small lounge. Your ticket and passport are scrutinized once more, and the ticket is matched against your checked luggage – another safety precaution. Finally, you are invited to board – and you are one step closer to the place you want to be – otherwise why are you travelling? On to the plane you walk, via an extension tunnel, or down the staircase, perhaps on to a short bus journey, and then up the portable steps. On entering the plane, the cabin crew welcome you, and direct you to your seat.

The flight

We are the present result of a process of evolution stretching back over millions of years, but in the twentieth century, technology started to develop almost uncomfortably quickly. This is particularly true of air travel. We have been forced to adapt, as in a relatively very short space of time it has become perfectly common to step into a machine and find ourselves whizzing through the air at 600 mph, tens of thousands of feet high in the sky. It is hardly surprising, therefore, that such new experiences take some getting used to. But, if flying seems against nature, it is really no more unnatural than travelling by car, or indeed all the other forms of transport that many people happily take for granted. True, flying can involve various unfamiliar experiences, so let us examine these one by one, going through the senses.

SMELLS

Walking up the stairs and on to the plane, you may notice the smell of aviation fuel. Like petrol for your car at the garage, this fuel has its own distinctive odour. As you step inside the aircraft, you probably will immediately notice that the air smells different. This is because the cabin air goes through the air conditioning system, and this gives a somewhat artificial smell. You will quickly get used to the atmosphere, even if it feels rather close to begin with. Entering the cabin, you could also become aware that the fire-resistant plastics used on board an aircraft also have a slight odour. Some people say they dislike this smell. Once again, the longer you are inside the cabin, the less likely you are to notice the unusual smell.

Once you get up to cruising height, i.e., the height at which the aircraft makes most of the journey (25,000–28,000 feet for shorter flights and 30,000–40,000 feet for longer ones), the amount of ozone in the air increases. This sometimes produces a noticeably strange smell, especially on long-distance flights and flights over the North Pole. Some people find it pleasant, while others experience it as an 'electric' or 'chlorine' smell. People who are sensitive to it sometimes complain of an oppressive feeling, a dry throat, or, very rarely, nosebleeds. However, a high ozone concentration seldom causes serious problems. In any case, modern wide-body jets (the ones with two aisles) are fitted with ozone filters.

The relatively dry air produced by the air conditioning can lead to dehydration, which may get worse if you drink lots of coffee or alcohol. It is a good idea to drink plenty of liquid, preferably fruit juice, milk, or water.

WHAT YOU SEE

When you step inside the aircraft you find yourself in a long tunnel full of seats, with small windows running down the length of the cabin on either side. Once you are sitting in your seat, the view forward is limited to the anonymous back of the seat in front you. To the left and right are other passengers, or on one side you may have the cabin wall with a window. Finally, above you, or on the armrest of your seat, is a panel with the controls for lighting and ventilation, and a crew call button. Through the window you get a traveller's eye view of the airport, as you are now 'airside', away from all those who would just love to be going with you!

Let's go over what you can see, in chronological order.

• Smoke-like condensation or maybe even a few drops of liquid often emerges from the ventilation openings. The condensation may make you think of fire, the drops of liquid of a leaking fuel pipe. In actual fact it is only condensation from the moist air that emerges from the air conditioning when the system is started. This happens especially in warm weather or in hot countries.

71

- In the pocket on the back of the seat in front of you, you will find information about what to do in an emergency, and it will show the location of the exits. Bus and train passengers are not given this information, but on aircrafts it is required by law. However, it is nothing to be worried about, as the chance of requiring it is – remember the statistic?

- The Fasten Seatbelts sign illuminates. Once again, this is a statutory requirement.

- The aircraft doors are shut and bolted. This can be a difficult moment if you suffer from claustrophobia. However, the ventilation and air condition system constantly supply more than enough fresh air, which is continually replaced. You will see the door close only if you are sitting in the nearby vicinity; otherwise you are unlikely to notice any difference in the cabin.

- The flight attendants walk along the rows of seats. No, they're not looking for something that's gone wrong; it is just another prescribed safety measure. They have to check that all the seats are upright, tray tables stowed, window blinds up and that all safety belts are fastened.

- Just before the aircraft starts to move, the cabin lights dim slightly for a moment and then return to full brightness. This happens when the auxiliary generator is switched off and the aircraft starts to draw its power from the thrust engines. The auxiliary generator, usually located at the rear of the craft, is powered by a separate engine not used for thrust.

- While the craft is taxiing towards the runway, you cannot see where you are going – your only view is out of the side window. This is when you particularly realize that you have to trust the pilots in the front cockpit; only they can see where the craft is heading.

- The flight attendants demonstrate the use of the oxygen masks, which automatically drop down if the cabin pressure falls. They also demonstrate the use of the lifejackets, which are stowed under the seats. The cabin crew members then go and sit beside the doors and emergency exits – yet another obligatory safety measure. If you are not aware that this is simply a precaution, you may start to imagine that something has gone wrong.

- During taxiing, the pilot checks the moving parts of the wings and extends the wing flaps. This can clearly be seen if you are sitting next to a window over the wing. This, too, forms part of the obligatory list of checks. If you are flying at night, the cabin lights are dimmed just before the take-off and then return to normal as soon as the plane is airborne. The reason is to allow your eyes to become adapted to the dark – yet another precaution solely aimed at ensuring your safety.

- There can be a long 'taxi' following the taxiway, which will take you to the runway that is to be used for take off. Often you may stop while other traffic feeds through. Remind yourself that the pilot is in control, and is under instruction over which route to take.

- During take-off the high acceleration causes a curious distortion of the view outside. Close by, the edge of the runway and the grassy strip beside it become blurred, while features further away remain clearly visible. In next to no time the aircraft is travelling as fast as a Formula One racing car, but the sensation of speed vanishes as soon as it leaves the ground.

- As we climb higher and higher above the earth, the landscape below us shrinks rapidly to Lilliputian

73

dimensions. At the same time, any connection between the speed that you see and the speed that you feel disappears entirely. Despite the view, it is difficult to orientate yourself with respect to the landscape. If this is your first flight, and you expected to be able to recognize the area round the airport, you will be surprised at not being able to tell where you are. In fact, it is remarkably difficult to pick out familiar features, certainly the first time.

- If you have a view of the rear of the wing, you will be able to see how the wing flaps retract once the aircraft has reached a safe height, i.e., a height at which the plane has more than enough space to reduce the angle of climb somewhat.

- Looking down from a great height – what some people may consider a dizzying height – you seem to be almost standing still, as if the plane is no longer moving forwards. If you are a newly fledged flyer, you may even imagine that the plane is falling, but eventually you will get used to this illusion. The motion of the aircraft with respect to the earth can be seen better if you look as straight down as possible. The feeling of not moving forwards sometimes also arises on a clear day when a large object, such as a high mountain, can be seen in the distance. Because you do not realize how far away the object actually is, it seems to come closer only very slowly.

- The 'Fasten Seatbelts' notice is switched off once the aircraft reaches a height of about 15,000 feet if the pilot does not expect any turbulence during the climb. This gives you the chance to go to the toilet, which feeds into the comforting idea that everything is going according to plan.

- While smoking used to be allowed, and there was a light in the overhead panel to indicate the times when it was permissible, the illuminated 'No Smoking' signs have now become outdated since almost universal bans on lighting up on scheduled passenger planes were introduced in the late 1990s; now, if there is a 'No Smoking' sign, it usually remains on for the duration of the flight.

- A recent development has enabled people to make calls on their mobile phones and send text messages. The new Airbus is being fitted with an overhead sign indicating times when it is permissible to use your mobile phone, and 'No Mobile' signs are planned to replace the outdated 'No Smoking' signs above airline seats with the likely future introduction of in-flight mobile phone services. The overhead 'No Mobile' signs are being retrofitted to older aircraft and fitted to the new Airbus planes coming off the production line, and these will be used by those airlines which provide an in-flight mobile phone service. The 'No Mobile' sign shows a mobile phone crossed out and is illuminated during take-off until the plane has reached a certain altitude in order to ensure there is no interference with mobile networks on the ground. After take-off, there will be an announcement that passengers are allowed to use their mobile phones. At this point the 'No Mobile' sign is turned off. The new signs initially have been only applicable to the smaller Airbus A320, A319 and 318 aircraft, but it is planned to have them on Boeing planes as well if the in-flight mobile service is extended to its aircraft in the future. Be aware that different airlines have different regulations concerning use of mobile phones. In early 2008, three passengers on an Alitalia flight were arrested when they refused to switch off their mobile phones!

- At certain heights and in some types of weather you may see liquid dripping from the wings. Don't worry – it is not leaking fuel; this is just water that condenses even out of clear air when moisture particles encounter the wings, which are ice-cold.

- You will have to get used to not being able to see the ground, as often it is obscured by the clouds above which you are flying. In fact, when the aircraft flies through clouds you cannot see anything at all.

- At some stage of the flight, the Fasten Seatbelts lights may come on again. This does not mean something is wrong; it is just a precaution when the pilot is flying through turbulent air, or when turbulence is expected. Sometimes it is even switched on to get the passengers back into their seats so the food and beverages can be served!

- For some people, nightmare seems to become reality when they see the wingtips moving up and down in unruly weather. The movement can actually be quite large: for example, the wingtips of a Boeing 747 can easily bend at least twelve feet in either direction. The wings are made to be bendy, in order to absorb upward and downward movements of the air. The wingtips have to be capable of moving up and down. Even the spire of Salisbury Cathedral sways in a high wind; it is this flexibility that prevents it from breaking.

- If you look around, you may see one of the cockpit crew strolling through the cabin. Again, there is no reason to be alarmed; while the aircraft is cruising, there is so little to do in the cockpit that one pilot can easily take care of the work.

- When the descent begins the Fasten Seatbelts (and possibly the 'No Mobile Phones' signs on those planes that allow mobiles at all) are switched on again. The flight attendants go and sit by the doors and emergency exits once more. As before, this is an obligatory safety precaution.

- Just as during take-off, the flaps are extended in order to give the wings more lift and enable the aircraft to fly more slowly.

- Just before landing, you may see the ground approaching rapidly, and the world returns to normal size once more. Looking through a window, it is difficult to estimate just when the aircraft will touch the ground, so you just have to sit and wait. At some airports all you can see is water until immediately just before touchdown, because the runway is beside the shore. It can be very difficult to judge height above water through a side window, unlike from the cockpit, where the pilots have clear vision to the front and sides, plus the information from their instruments.

SOUNDS

The sound level in the cabin of commercial airliner in flight is 35–85 decibels: sixty-five decibels is comparable to normal street noise, while 100 decibels corresponds to the level of noise in the machine room of a ship. These days, aircraft designers are managing to limit the noise from the engines and have been increasingly able to prevent it from entering the cabin.

Noise is one of the things that can cause feelings of fear. The constant din can sound even louder when one is frightened, and, together with worries about what is happening, can leave one feeling totally exhausted, particularly on a long flight. Fear also occurs when people who are nervous about flying hear noises that they cannot place in a familiar context: unusual, sometimes sudden noises that often cannot be recognized. What you hear depends to a certain extent on where you sit on the plane.

Let's go through all the noises, one by one.

- If you hear banging and thumping when you get into the aircraft, that is usually the noise of luggage and freight being loaded into the hold.
- If you are sitting next to the door, at a certain moment you will hear an alarm signal. This is simply to let the cabin personnel know that a tractor has towed away the steps, or that the mobile corridor (through which passengers enter the plane) has been retracted, so that the aircraft doors can be closed.
- As you enter the cabin, you sometimes hear an insistent, slightly hissing noise, which comes from the air conditioning or ventilation.
- You may hear a whine or whirring noise coming from the turbine that drives the auxiliary generator.
- The engines are started up one by one. This briefly demands a lot of power, so that the hissing and blowing of the air conditioning lessens.
- In order to start taxiing, the pilot has to boost the engines a little in order to get the aircraft moving; as soon as the plane is rolling, the engines run slower once more.
- A warning signal, 'ding-dong', sounds when the Fasten Seatbelts sign come on. You will hear it again at various times during the flight, whenever these signs are switched on or off. A similar signal is heard

when a passenger presses the button in order to call a flight attendant, or when a flight attendant wishes to call a colleague. You may be startled to hear this signal while the aircraft is cruising, because you expect it to be followed by an announcement. The same signal is indeed used both when the pilot wishes to tell the cabin crew something or to make an announcement to the passengers. This sound is part of the normal activity, and does not signify anything unusual, or that there is anything amiss.

- When the engines run up to full power during take-off, some passengers imagine that the aircraft is about to explode. The sudden increase in engine noise is impressive, but quite normal.

- Sometimes you may hear a rumble or feel a vibration when you are travelling along the runway. It helps to think of it in the same way as you do when your car is travelling over a bumpy road.

- Once the aircraft has left the ground, you may hear a 'whump' as the wheels are automatically braked before being retracted. The noise of the brake depends on the type of aircraft. Sometimes, instead of the 'whump', there may be a slightly longer, dull thudding sound as the wheels are retracted; this is caused by a rubber block being pressed against the wheels. If you listen carefully, you can even hear the suspension dropping as the wheels part contact with the runway.

- A dull thud may be heard from underneath the cock-pit, caused by the nose wheel being retracted, and during approximately the next twenty seconds there is the whine of the other wheels being retracted. The undercarriage is retracted in order to streamline the underside of the aircraft.

- When the aircraft has been in the air for barely a minute, you may have the impression that the engines are stopping, as the noise decreases so dramatically. In fact, this means the pilot has throttled back because he has been given permission by the control tower to fly briefly at a low altitude before climbing further. Shortly afterwards, the engines resume full power for the climb, and the noise level duly rises.

- If you are sitting beside a door, you may hear a high-pitched whistling noise that gradually fades away as the aircraft gains height. By about 7,500 feet it vanishes entirely. This is due to the lowering of the air pressure in the cabin, and once again is perfectly normal.

- A well-known phenomenon during ascent or descent is the 'popping' of the ears. Some people are already familiar with this sound (which is actually more of a feeling) from car travel in the mountains, or when travelling by cable car. However, someone who has never encountered it before can get quite a fright, especially since it can sometimes seem as if you are going deaf. Yawning widely, sucking on a sweet, or swallowing helps it to go away. The phenomenon is caused by the difference in air pressure inside and outside your eardrum. For technical reasons, it is not possible to maintain the same pressure in the cabin as at ground level. The pressure in the cabin is gradually reduced until it is equivalent to what you experience in the mountains at a height of 6,000 feet. The pressure then stays at this level for the remainder of the flight, even when cruising above 30,000 feet. In a few rare cases, the pressure difference can lead to stimulation of the facial nerve, causing temporary pain, or to problems with one's eardrums.

- At cruising height there is a constant 'whishing' sound, since the noise of the air outside is no longer drowned by the engines.
- Once the descent begins, the engines are throttled back and so make less noise while the aircraft glides downwards.
- The wing flaps are extended using an electric motor, which can be heard in the neighbourhood of the wings.
- During the descent, the pressure gradually rises again, so that you hear/feel your ears popping once more, and the temporary deafness returns. The popping is more marked on the descent than on the ascent.
- There is a bang as the undercarriage doors in the belly of the aircraft open. This is followed by the whine of the undercarriage being extended, lasting for about twenty seconds.
- You can hear the rumble of the wheels once they touch the ground.
- Once all the wheels – including the nose wheel – are on the ground, the engines suddenly start to howl as the thrust is reversed. At the same time, the speed brakes on the wings are raised, in order to reduce the braking distance of the aircraft.

WHAT YOU FEEL

The movements of the aircraft can also be unsettling for inexperienced passengers. Most movement is felt during take-off and landing.

- In the first instance, the plane, which is usually parked nose first towards the terminal building, has to be towed away from its stand. You therefore feel a jolt go through the aircraft, which then starts to move backwards as it is pushed back away from the pier. An aircraft cannot move backwards under its own power; it has to be pushed by a tractor to a point where it can start taxiing forward.

- A slight vibration goes through the aircraft from front to rear, as the engines are started up one by one.
- The aircraft may bump along at first as it starts to taxi. A great deal of engine power is necessary to get such a heavy mass moving. Once the aircraft is rolling along, the power is throttled back.
- As the engines run up to full speed for the take-off, a vibration goes through the fuselage from front to rear.
- The acceleration pushes you back in your seat.
- As the aircraft climbs, you may feel it dip slightly now and then. This is a normal result of the wing flaps being retracted in stages. In reality, the aircraft does not dip; it only feels like that to your balance perception. A climbing turn can cause a strange feeling in your head and in the pit of your stomach. If you feel this, don't worry, you are not the only one. It may feel strange, but it is perfectly harmless.
- If you are attentive, you may notice the changes in course and altitude during the flight.
- You may feel a sudden vibration, or even bumps, going through the whole aircraft. This is caused by turbulence, i.e., irregular motion of the air. Usually, commercial aircraft fly so high that they are 'above the weather', and so are hardly affected by turbulence. Sometimes, however, 'clear-air turbulence' may occur at high altitude. As its name implies, this form of turbulence cannot be seen by the pilots beforehand,

and therefore advance warning to fasten your seatbelt may not be given. While it may be uncomfortable, it is nothing to worry about. Just think of it as similar to a bus travelling over a bumpy road. Turbulence more usually occurs at lower altitudes, during the ascent or descent. It is generally produced by temperature variations in the air, and is nearly always felt when the aircraft is flying through clouds. The aircraft is designed to deal with this, and can easily withstand the shocks produced by turbulence, thanks to its built-in resilience. Turbulence is often referred to colloquially as 'hitting an air pocket', conjuring up visions for the anxious passenger of flying into a vacuum or a 'hole in the air'. However, such a thing is physically impossible. You may have the impression of falling, but this is due not so much to loss of height as loss of speed due to the variation in air flow. What you have to bear in mind is that air is far from being 'nothing'; air is for an aircraft as water is for a boat. In this book we have devoted a separate section to turbulence, just to make certain that you as a passenger are properly informed about it.

• Inexperienced passengers may be alarmed if the aircraft seems to be circling repeatedly in the same direction, and they may start imagining that the pilot has lost his way. All that has happened in reality is that the plane is in the vicinity of the airport, and that air traffic control has ordered the pilot to fly a 'holding pattern', in the shape of a race track, until permission can be given to land. The size of the track varies with the speed of the plane as each circuit of the track shape takes exactly four minutes to complete.

• On some flights the descent can be rougher than the ascent, because the pilot has been ordered to fly more slowly. This is accomplished by means of 'speed brakes', or flaps that are extended to slow the aircraft down. Depending on the type of aircraft, these brakes may be situated on the main wings (in which case they may cause slight turbulence) or they may be mounted on the tail (in which case you will hardly notice anything).

- During the runway approach, the wing profile is modified; the wing surface is increased by extending the flaps, which sometimes makes the motion of the aircraft rougher. Also, the air can become more turbulent closer to the ground.

- The descent begins gradually, but at some point the aircraft may seem to halt its descent. Don't worry; the pilot is simply following orders from air traffic control.

- When the aircraft touches down, you feel a bump as the wheels hit the ground, followed by vibration (although the landing gear absorbs most of the shudder). You feel a braking force, which seems to push you forward in your seat, as the engines switch to reverse thrust and the brakes are applied to the wheels. If the runway is wet, you can expect a slightly harder landing. This is done quite deliberately, in order to prevent aquaplaning. The purpose is to break through the layer of water and get the wheels turning on the tarmac. But a harder landing does not mean a less safe landing; in fact, quite the contrary – the pilots know exactly what they are doing.

SENSE OF BALANCE

In comparison with most other means of transport (submarines excluded!), an aircraft is more varied in its motions. It not only travels left and right, but also up and down. Of course, it also goes forwards, and even goes backwards when towed away from the stand where it is usually parked nose-first. Our sense of balance keeps us aware of these movements. The balance organ lies in the vestibule of the inner ear, close to the auditory apparatus. It has two parts: a fixed organ and three semicircular canals filled with fluid. The function of our balance organ is to keep us aware of the position, acceleration and motion of our body.

Our eyes also play an important part in gathering relevant data. Yet more data is provided by the muscles and bones of our bodies, which report to the brain on the degree of contraction and the pressure on the body. The brain processes all this data and translates it into information about the position of the body. Unfortunately, the brain has difficulty in distinguishing between tension and compression caused by changes in the position of the body, and tension and compression caused by changes in the force of gravity. In an aircraft, the flight motions and high accelerations can interfere with gravitational force.

What happens when our brains receive data from our sensory organs, but these data do not seem to agree with each other? Scientists have found that in such a situation, people orientate themselves purely by what they see: sight enjoys priority over other senses. But, except during take-off and landing, or when flying low in clear weather, passengers in an aircraft have hardly any way of telling whether what they see or feel agrees with reality. For those not sitting beside a window there is no possibility at all. This is probably why most people prefer a window seat. Some nervous flyers do not experience any problems as long as they have a good view. By contrast, there are those who refuse to sit beside a window, for fear of vertigo. Due to this lack of visual information, in an aircraft we are almost completely dependent on what our balance organ tells us. However, the system has its limits: the semi-circular canals perceive movements in space, but are not sensitive to very slight movements (less than 3° per second). This means that if an aircraft banks into a turn more slowly than 3° per second, you have the impression that it is still flying level. If the pilot then rights the aircraft more quickly (faster than 3° per second), you 'feel' as if the plane is banking and continuing to turn, whereas in fact it is flying level once more. To give another example, when the aircraft climbs gently for a certain length of time, from, for example, 6,000 to 30,000 feet, your balance organ does not sense this; and you assume the plane is flying horizontally. When the pilot then levels out at 30,000 feet, it feels as if the plane has started to dive. This can be a worrying experience, because you are left wondering why the aircraft is losing height. Changes in balance are felt mainly during landing and take-off, and during changes in course and altitude, turbulence, and airport approaches/departures.

When the sense of balance is disturbed by single or repeated movements, whether expected or unexpected, this can cause travel sickness in people who are susceptible to it. This can happen not just in an aircraft, but also in a car, bus, train, boat, and certain fairground rides. It is a common misconception that you will never experience travel sickness if you can see the movement coming, without being passively subject to it. However, people who are particularly susceptible to travel sickness can delay its onset, and may sometimes avoid it altogether, by anticipating the movement as much as possible, instead of submitting to it passively. This means actively going along with the movement, leaning into the bends, and, in case of turbulence, behaving as if you are causing the movement yourself. In an aircraft, however, the possibilities for your anticipating the movements are very limited. Fortunately, there are effective medications against travel sickness, and taking these is unlikely to lead to tolerance or dependence.

Additional factors

In addition to the above, there are various other things that can make you as a passenger feel uncomfortable. You have to get used to the very limited freedom of movement that you have. You can go to the toilet only occasionally. Certainly, you can recline your seat, but many people prefer not to, because they think that this may interfere with the passenger behind them, and they do not want to do this.

Under normal circumstances, each person has their own preferred 'personal space' around him or her, i.e., the limit that determines how close other, strange people are allowed to come. The actual distance depends on our mood, our personality, and our culture. On board an aircraft, however, little or no allowance is made for this; we can feel ourselves seriously restricted, and perhaps feel that our personal space is being invaded, or even violated. The reality is that room on board is very limited, and has to be used as economically as possible.

Sitting too long in one position causes a build up of pressure in the blood vessels in the thighs; and this can make the veins in the feet and ankles swell up, and shoes start to pinch. After a certain length of time you may start to feel stiff. Airlines capitalize on this by vying with each other about the amount of space offered to passengers. Usually, though, this happens for the more expensive classes of seating. You can make yourself more comfortable during a flight by unlacing, unbuckling, or removing your shoes. There is also no reason why you should not take a walk along the aisle to stretch your legs once the aircraft is cruising.

You may feel in a helpless position in relation to the cabin crew, and dependent on their mercy. All you feel you can do is let them take care of you. And indeed they do: they offer drinks, serve meals, and in general do everything they can to make passengers feel comfortable. However, eating and drinking can be rather a tricky business when the aircraft experiences turbulent weather (in fact, just as tricky as eating and drinking on a bus driving along a bumpy road). If the turbulence gets too severe, the flight attendants may even decide that it is better not to serve anything. This may be inconvenient, but it is certainly nothing to get worried about.

On longer flights, entertainment is usually provided in the form of films and audio programmes. Increasingly, there is a wider choice, available on demand, even for economy passengers. Catching up with new films, and even the classic ones, can help pass the time. It is important to remind yourself that the engine sounds are the responsibility of the pilot – your assistance in monitoring them really is not needed!

If your body is in normal condition, this will help you begin to relax comfortably during the flight. It is strongly recommended not to drink alcohol. The lower air pressure on board an aircraft makes you intoxicated more quickly. Furthermore, alcohol – like coffee – tends to have a dehydrating effect. It is a good idea to drink more liquid than usual, but be sparing with alcohol and coffee.

People with a bad cold, or who are developing a sinus infection, should be careful about flying; in such a case it might be better not to fly at all, since you have to withstand a pressure difference equivalent to 6,000 feet of altitude. You would have just as much trouble travelling by car from sea level to 6,000 feet up in the mountains. It is also a good idea to be careful about what you eat before flying, since the drop in pressure can result in intestinal gases expanding, with all the discomfort that this brings. Foods that can lead to gas formation in the intestines include onions, cabbage, raw apples, radishes, beans, pea soup, cucumber, and melon.

After landing

Once the aircraft has taxied to a stop, people frequently start to get out of their seats despite the fact that the Fasten Seatbelts sign is still on. This is against the regulations. If you remain seated, as instructed, it is likely to be less unpleasant than standing up and being hemmed in by all those people in the aisle. This is especially the case if you have a tendency to feel claustrophobic. In any case, there is no point in standing up, as you cannot leave the aircraft until:

- you hear the announcement from the cockpit, 'Cabin crew, yellow door selectors', or 'Cabin crew, door selectors manual', or 'Cabin crew, doors from automatic';
- the engines have been shut down;
- the Fasten Seatbelts sign is switched off;
- you hear the announcement from the cockpit, 'Cabin crew, doors can be opened';

- the boarding corridor has been extended from the gate to the aircraft and the doors have been opened. If the airport does not have modern boarding corridors, then you will have to wait until steps have been placed against the aircraft;
- the passengers in the seats in front of you have gathered up their hand luggage and cleared the aisle.

Once all the above has taken place, you can then collect your own hand luggage at your leisure and leave the aircraft. Quite probably you will not be familiar with the place where you have landed, and will be faced by a whole series of new experiences. Inside the terminal building, you will have to show your passport to the Immigration Officers. There may also be an Immigration Form to hand in, and some countries ask for a visa or a valid vaccination certificate, which is normally obtained before you travel. You then proceed to the baggage collection point. All the luggage will be found on an identified moving belt, known as a carousel. Having identified and claimed your own luggage, you then proceed through the Customs area. The formalities can sometimes take a while. You may have to hand in another form, or permit your luggage to be searched.

Out you go into the Arrivals Hall, to enjoy the next part of your trip. It can make a difference whether you are travelling alone or with company, and whether you are being met at the airport or have to find your own way. It is worth planning in advance how you are going to get from the airport to your destination, as this means you will experience considerably less stress, as you will know what you have to do. Bear in mind that the climate may be very different from what you are used to at home, and have appropriate clothing in your hand luggage, so you can either cool down or warm up accordingly. Wherever you are, keep a close eye on your luggage: unfortunately, thieves are everywhere!

Jet lag, or the impact of the time difference

On long flights, tiredness is one of the hazards to be faced. There is a phenomenon that adds to the tiredness if you fly from one time zone to another and cross a number of time zones: your body cannot adjust quickly enough to the different rhythms of night and day. It does not matter whether you fly from east to west, or from west to east. In both cases, you will probably cross a number of time zones, or even the International Date Line. This leads to what is popularly known as 'jet lag'. It does not affect you if you fly from north to south or vice versa, because then there is no time zone crossing involved. Of course, after having to sit in an aircraft seat for a long time, plus all the excitement of the trip, you may naturally already feel somewhat tired. You can usually get over this fatigue with a good night's sleep. However, when this is compounded with jet lag, it becomes somewhat more complicated (Figure 8).

Time zones

The phrase 'jet lag' was coined by the Americans and describes how our biological and psychological rhythms lag behind the actual time. The rhythms are disturbed because we pass through various time zones when we travel by jet plane. The fact that we are travelling at great speed and high altitude has nothing to do with this; the

Time zones

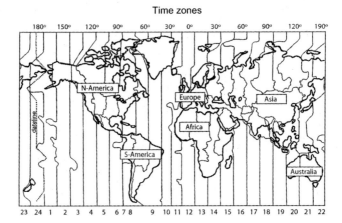

Figure 8. Map showing time zones.

effect of the speed is only incidental, in that you are whisked from one time zone to another.

When you land in a different time zone, you have to adjust your watch. However, resetting the body's internal clock is not so easy. The human body has its own biological clock, or rather a large number of clocks, all running at different speeds but meshing with each other like gearwheels. These mechanisms regulate the working of the organs in our body, controlling the hormone levels, the blood pressure, the body's temperature, the digestion, the operation of the kidneys, the bladder function, the heartbeat, and the brainwave pattern. The internal or biological clock appears to adapt only slowly and takes a while to get back into phase with the time differences. The biological clock resides in the suprachiasmatic core of the brain, and consists of two parts which each play a different role. The bottom half reacts immediately to light that comes in through the eyes, but the upper half reacts indirectly and needs several days to adapt. Recently, it has been

92

discovered at Leiden University that the neurotransmitter GABA plays an important role in this adjustment.

A prerequisite for feeling normal is for your bodily rhythms to be in step with the actual rhythm of night and day. When you travel eastwards or westwards, you cross from one time zone to another and so land in a different sequence of night and day. The result is that your body thinks it is still night, while outside it is quite clearly day, or vice versa.

Fortunately, our internal clock is able to adapt to the new rhythm, but not quite as fast as a jet travels. Your bio-rhythm can adapt by approximately two hours in every twenty-four-hour period. The various bodily mechanisms all take a different length of time to adapt. It is interesting to note that babies under three months do not suffer from jet lag; they keep blissfully to their own pattern of eating and sleeping, independent of night and day. Several functions in the human body depend on the circadian rhythm. The word circadian comes from 'circa', which means approximately, and 'dia', meaning day.

This rhythm is dictated by the influence of a hormone, melatonin, which is secreted by the pineal gland, a pea-shaped organ in the centre of the brain. The gland begins to secrete melatonin when it becomes dark at night, and stops when it becomes light in the morning. The production of this hormone is at its lowest around eight in the morning and increases around ten at night. The greatest production is at around two o'clock at night. All kinds of circadian rhythms are controlled by melatonin, and this hormone is an important sleep regulator.

The effects of jet lag are more pronounced if you fly from east to west than if you fly in the opposite direction. Flights to destinations far to the east, such as Tokyo from

London, are the most troublesome from the point of view of jet lag. The body has difficulty in accommodating the greatly shortened day. A difference of four time zones generally does not cause any real bother, but various jet lag symptoms start to appear from the fifth time zone onwards. Each time zone covers a period of one hour.

Research is still being carried out into the effects, and there is still a lot to find out about them. Symptoms that can appear directly after arrival as a result of jet lag include the following: tiredness, fatigue, difficulty in orientating, reduced alertness, confusion, disturbed eating pattern, loss of memory, sensitivity to cold due to a fall in body temperature, and irregular urges to urinate or defecate.

You may also notice some of the following symptoms a few days after arrival in a new time zone: constipation/diarrhoea, reduced sexual appetite, increased muscle tension, night blindness, reduced physical performance, disturbed body rhythms, delayed reaction to what is seen, slower reflexes, possible changes in the effects of prescribed medication, insomnia, acute tiredness, lack of appetite, and headaches. It is important to be aware that the symptoms of jet lag are generally of a temporary nature only. However, if we are tense and nervous, various other hormones can be secreted that further disturb the biological clock, so the calmer you stay, the less problem you will have with jet lag.

People suffering from jet lag can be less effective when taking decisions, and this could lead to unwelcome consequences. For this reason, some companies forbid their employees to take important business decisions on the day of arrival after a long flight east or west. Should someone make a bad decision as a result of jet lag, they could face problems, and as a result could develop an aversion to flying, or even a flying phobia. However, it is not the flying that causes the tiredness and discomfort, but simply the fact of crossing time zones, and this is something for which allowance should be made.

You can try in various ways to limit the impact of jet lag by following the advice listed below.

- Make sure you are fit before you begin the journey. The evening before the flight, drink a glass of warm milk before you go to sleep. Warm milk contains tryptophan, a substance that helps to maintain good day-and-night rhythm. During the flight, settle comfortably into your seat, if possible with the legs slightly raised, for example by using something as a foot-rest. Periodically relax your feet and legs, and flex your calf muscles. Doing little exercises like these helps to prevent the body becoming stiff.

- Do not wait until you arrive to adjust your watch; set it to the destination time on departure. That way, you produce a psychological pre-synchronization effect.

- Eat only moderate amounts on board, and do not drink any alcohol. For the midday meal, eat plenty of protein (meat, fish, cheese, or grain products), and for the evening meal give preference to carbohydrates (rice, pasta, or potatoes). This will help you to relax and adjust.

- Take enough liquid, by drinking lots of water, fruit juices, milk, or lemonade. But remember: no alcohol or coffee. Caffeine produces an increase in brain activity and that is not what we want when we are trying to sleep. The effect can last for several hours before the caffeine is finally excreted from our system, therefore the impact of a high consumption of coffee, or cola, can mean that one stays up all night.

- Try to sleep during the flight, especially on a night flight. On a day flight, take a nap before and after lunch, and on a night flight try to sleep immediately. In fact, the golden rule for any night flight is, get as much rest as possible!

- The drug 'melatonin' has become very popular as an aid to help with sleeping problems. There is further discussion about this below, and we do not recommend that it be taken. The best recommendation is still to live and work according to the natural cycle of day and night wherever you are, and to follow a normal, healthy diet.

- Light therapy against jet lag appears to be a very effective and is increasingly being utilized.

- Try to adjust to the new situation as quickly as possible. As soon as you have landed, take account of the light, the time, the temperature, and all the other conditions of your destination. When you arrive at your hotel, if you feel cold, take a hot shower in order to raise your body temperature.

- Remain active if it is daytime at your destination, and rest or sleep at the usual times for that place. In short, behave like the local people in the destination country. Eat the local food, where it is considered safe, and keep to the local times for meals.

- Go to bed early, and take measures to ensure that your sleep is not disturbed by hunger pangs during the night. For example, find out if your hotel has room service. If need be, order in a snack in case you wake up feeling hungry during the night.

- Be on your guard: physiologically, you may need a few days for your internal clock to get back 'in synch' and for you to be on top form, especially, for instance, when you have come from the West to Tokyo. So do not let yourself be talked into signing an important contract on the day of your arrival.

- Take a few breaks in your schedule by strolling in the grounds of your hotel, or taking just a little time to look around before letting yourself get immersed in business.

People who are troubled by the negative effects of jet lag frequently report that they have tried a vast array of methods to alleviate their symptoms. These include taking melatonin, doing yoga, or following a special diet. Unfortunately, nothing really seems to be totally effective in eradicating the problem.

Although melatonin can be a corrector of sleep and it has not been found to have any significant side effects, we nevertheless recommend using it only periodically. Recent research studies from professional pilot organizations have found that there is the possibility of loss of concentration, memory, and vigilance during the day when using melatonin. At present, there are insufficient extended period studies with conclusive evidence about the long-term effects.

There are also more natural ways to keep your melatonin production at the right level: for example, by living and working as much as possible according to the ordinary cycle of day and night. The most important piece of advice, therefore, is to adjust to the cycle of day and night at your destination as best you can, and as quickly as possible. As soon as you are able, once you reach your destination, try to put yourself in a place where there is daylight.

CHAPTER THREE

THE EXERCISES, OR HOW TO EXORCIZE YOUR FEARS

Learning new skills

This chapter describes our method for overcoming fear of flying on your own. It is not a magic remedy: you will not get rid of flying phobia just by reading this chapter, unless you put the instructions into practice. Nevertheless, the method has a very good chance of success if you follow it seriously for a month or two, spending at least ten or fifteen minutes on it per day, four or five times per week.

How quickly you can get over your fear of flying varies from person to person; and depends on the severity of the phobia, as well as the type. The do-it-yourself method may not be sufficient for every nervous flyer. To find out whether or not this applies to you, try to answer the following questions as honestly as possible.

Ask yourself the following question: is it really flying that you are afraid of, or does this fear serve as a cover for something else? If you have to admit that the latter is the case, you should first try to tackle the main problem. Whatever the problem is, whether you can deal with it by yourself or not, there is bound to be a better solution than avoiding plane journeys. If these exercises do not prove sufficient to overcome your difficulties, you may benefit from professional help, perhaps from a clinical psychologist. Later in this book we will examine the types of professional help available.

The chapter covers information about thoughts and behaviour, as well as examining breathing.

Self-help exercises are then explained. They provide strategies on how to restore your self-confidence, which can then enable you to enjoy relaxed air travel. Each of these strategies has to be mastered and put into practice; you have to apply each one conscientiously and systematically, in order to achieve the desired result. Read the following pages carefully, and then start to put what they tell you into practice. You may feel that you cannot accomplish all these steps unaided, which is perfectly understandable. In such a case, do not hesitate to seek professional help or support.

The method consists of three steps, which are first practised individually and then combined. As has already been mentioned, there is far less chance of fear if you are in a physically good condition and relaxed, so this is the first thing that you should try to achieve. Fear and tension go together, and since tension and relaxation are the opposite of one another, you can start to deal with fear by relaxing. It is therefore very important for you to be able to relax in any situation. There are some simple exercises for doing this.

As previously mentioned, when we are afraid or alarmed, we usually tense many muscles without realizing it. This also happens if we are worried or anxious about something, or if we are particularly attentive and alert. If we continually tense our muscles when this is not really necessary, we put an extra load on our body, which can lead to physical complaints, tiredness, and irritability. It is, therefore, a good idea to completely relax our bodies now and then. If you are relaxed, you will feel better emotionally and physically.

Tension also affects our respiration; we all know how we hold our breath, or breathe in sharply, in certain situations. It is, therefore, important during the relaxation exercise to breathe in deeply, and in particular to breathe out slowly and calmly.

Good, complete relaxation cannot be achieved by simply sitting quietly in a chair. The method below teaches you how to relax as many muscles as possible. While the method described here is perfectly sound, you can of course also practise other relaxation techniques that you happen to know. For example, if you do yoga, you can use those techniques.

There are various ways of utilizing the relaxation instructions below. You can record them on tape, speaking the text yourself at a relaxed rate, and then play it back to yourself. After a while you will know the text by heart, and will be able to carry the exercises out step by step without needing to listen to the recording. Alternatively, you can ask somebody else to read the text aloud for you, or record them doing so, and once again practise until you have mastered the method and can do the exercise by yourself.

When you're cool, calm, and collected

As we all know, when we are at ease, relaxed and just breathing gently, our view of the world usually reflects this, so that the world itself seems a more peaceful place. This perspective also applies to flying! Therefore, it is important to learn how to relax physically prior to the flight and during the flight itself. A lot of people are often not aware that they are physically tense both when thinking about travelling by air, or during the flight itself. Although others see that they are tense, they are not able to tell which part of their body is the most tense. Sometimes they also do not notice changes in their way of breathing. As in all situations, when we fail to recognize, or even deny, being tense, or are unaware of when tension occurs, perhaps at a specific time before or during a particular part of the flight, we are unable to do anything about it.

We notice muscle tension when it causes unpleasant feelings in our bodies; for instance, a headache or back pain. And if you are suffering from pain or tension, you are more liable to become anxious and it will also make you tired. Perhaps the worst of all is the fact that when your muscles are tense, you automatically resist the movements of the aircraft. This exacerbates the experience of the movement caused by turbulence. But the good news is, relaxation is something you can learn! If you do, the pent-up anxiety can start to disappear. A good way of learning relaxation is a technique called progressive relaxation.

The progressive relaxation technique is an important, commonly used, and easy to learn method of relaxation. It is called 'progressive' because it involves progressively relaxing more and more muscles. If you manage to keep the tension in your muscles consistently low (or at least lower) instead of consistently high, this not only affects the muscles themselves but also the state of your whole body. This in turn can lead to important changes in your state of mind, so that you feel generally much better. However, it is important to remember that this progressive relaxation technique has lasting beneficial effects only if it is practised regularly. 'Regularly' means, if possible, once per day before going on a trip by air. Do not practise only when you feel tense and nervous, but also on days when you feel calm and relaxed.

In order to become aware of any tensed muscles, it is advisable to learn to relax your whole body. Therefore, we describe in this chapter progressive relaxation exercises that will help you to learn how to relax. As previously mentioned, there are a variety of ways to do this, and we suggest you experiment to find out what works best for you. The alternatives include making your own recording of the exercises, or asking some one else to do this for you. You can play back the recording to direct your relaxation practice. Regular practice is important, and over time you will be able to reduce the length of the exercise as you learn to relax more quickly.

Without training, it is particularly difficult not to be tense when you are afraid. It is, therefore, necessary to practise relaxation in advance, as well as in the situations you find difficult or frightening.

Practise regularly, without rushing the exercises. Find a place where you feel comfortable and where you will not be disturbed. Perhaps you are already familiar with relaxation techniques. If not, you should realize that you are learning a new skill, and that this takes time. Later, you will be able to find plenty of opportunities for putting what you have learned into practice. Our advice is to practise on a regular basis and be aware that breathing plays an important role in the relaxation techniques.

As mentioned at the beginning of this chapter, when you are anxious, not only does the tension change in various muscle groups, but also your breathing pattern alters. If you are frightened, you begin to breathe faster. Many people fail to notice that, when on board an aircraft, they breathe differently because they are tense or anxious. The increased rate of breathing can cause physical symptoms, such as a racing heart, tingling in the hands and feet, and dizziness. Fortunately, it is possible to do something about these unpleasant phenomena. You can start to get them under control fairly quickly by correcting your rate of breathing and your level of muscle tension. Although fundamentally this is not difficult, the tips in this chapter will be of help to make it even easier. Take the time to read through the breathing exercises.

Let us take a closer look at what happens when you breathe. Concentrate on your respiration and become aware of your own particular way of breathing. Take a few deep breaths.

With each breath, we take oxygen into the body. The oxygen enters the blood through the lungs, and is carried by the blood to all parts of the body. The cells in our bodies use oxygen to produce energy. The waste products – mostly carbon dioxide – are carried away by the blood to the lungs, and expelled to the outside air when we breathe out. Usually, we are quite unaware of this process, although, as we all know, our lives depend on it. Fortunately, however, respiration continues whether we pay attention to it or not. Nevertheless, it is important to realize that this bodily function can be brought under conscious control to a large extent.

Shallow breathing

Chest, or high, breathing is relatively shallow. When you take a chest breath, your rib cage expands and your shoulders lift as your lungs take in air. When we are tense, we all have a tendency to breathe shallowly. Respiration often becomes irregular, partly because we hold our breath and do not allow ourselves time to breathe out completely. This pattern quickly leads to a feeling of suffocation. This, of course, is unpleasant, and can even give you the idea that you are not getting enough oxygen, which in itself is reason enough to panic. If you are limiting yourself to shallow respiration, you may develop complaints such as shortness of breath and tightness in the chest.

Abdominal breathing

A better way of breathing is to try to concentrate on your lower stomach, and use the diaphragm, a large, upward-curving sheet of muscle stretching over the bottom of your lungs and separating them from the abdominal organs. When we breathe in with the diaphragm, this muscle contracts and moves downwards, pulling air into our lungs. When we breathe out, employing the deliberate use of our diaphragm to breathe, we can change the shallow pattern of chest breathing and so improve our respiration. Abdominal breathing is important while flying because it is a simple way of reducing anxiety and tension and because there is slightly less oxygen in the cabin air, though this still equates to the amount you have when in a winter sports ski resort.

Given that we usually do not pay attention to the way in which we breathe, it may initially be confusing to concentrate on your breathing, as it is a process which has always been subconscious. By making it conscious, it is suddenly experienced as new and strange. Such a reaction is perfectly normal. With practice and patience, most people can learn to breathe in a relaxed manner.

105

Behaviour: it ain't what you do, it's the way that you do it

When driven by fear, people often behave in a different way. These fear-inspired habits may be quite unconscious, and frequently they are of no help to the sufferers but, on the contrary, make them feel worse. People with fear of flying say that during anxious moments they behave in a way that they recognize as a habit, although it is certainly not a conscious choice on their part. They may realize afterwards how they behaved, but at the moment itself they seem to have no other choice. In some cases the person may be well aware that their behaviour is not making the situation any better, in fact is making it worse, but they usually say 'I couldn't help it!'

Examples of behaviour that frequently occur include bracing oneself during take-off or landing; 'helping to brake' during the landing by pushing back against the seat and bracing your feet against the floor or the seat in front; and trying to make yourself as 'light' as possible during turbulence by sitting 'lightly' on your seat, raising the feet from the floor or sitting on one buttock. The only result is to make your stomach muscles as hard as Rocky Marciano's! The pilots do not feel any of this 'help': the only person who feels anything is you and it does not help you one little bit. Another example is when you sit motionless in your seat, without daring to stand up, even when you really have to go to the toilet or fetch something from your hand luggage. However you move – or don't move – it does not affect the aircraft in the slightest way.

Mary was a thirty-two-year-old medical assistant who never relaxed in her seat during take-off, because she wanted to make herself as light as possible in order to help the pilots and the aircraft itself, so as to make the take-off easier and safer. She never enjoyed taking off; in fact, it was always the worst part of the flight for her. During therapy we asked her what was her weight (not a very polite question to a lady) and she replied 'ten stone'. She was then asked to carry out behaviours that would reduce her weight to five stone! At that, she began laughing. In the plane itself she was asked to make herself as limp and loose as possible during the take-off, with as much concentration as possible, so that afterwards she could remember what she had done. This was a completely new experience in her flying life. Three minutes after take-off she was asked to stop concentrating on the exercise, and she admitted excitedly that the take-off had been the most enjoyable of her life.

Another example is that of Harry. He was a forty-eight-year-old businessman who regularly had to fly, but who increasingly tried to avoid it because he was always left with terrible muscular pain after the flight. During the flight within the therapy, it quickly became clear what the problem was: right from take-off, he braced himself as if he wanted to lift the aircraft clear of the ground by brute force. He clamped his hands fast on the armrests, and did his utmost to pull himself upwards, seat and all. Once in the air he relaxed a little, but you could see how his muscles tensed with every movement of the aircraft, even the slightest shake. His hands in particular had a hard time; he clenched them into tight fists, so hard that they were completely red and became wet with perspiration. It was obvious then that he would behave in the same way during the landing. It was therefore suggested that he hold a plastic cup in each hand while the plane was landing. When leaving the aircraft, he looked at the pathetic remains of the plastic cups and he had to laugh at himself: they looked like shredded scraps of paper.

During the return flight he held a plastic cup in each hand, and he was asked to try to keep them both whole. Just after take-off, when the tension had relaxed somewhat, Harry proudly showed his right hand, with the cup in pristine condition. Unfortunately, the result in his left hand was disappointing; he had made such an effort to concentrate on his right hand that he had failed to notice that his left hand was crunching up its plastic cup.

For landing, two new cups were produced, and Harry said he was determined to try to avoid falling into his 'hold habit'. Landing used to be the most difficult time for Harry. But this time he was more successful, and he realized how deeply rooted was the habit. He also understood that it was not the aircraft that caused the muscular pain, but his own exertions and useless feats of strength. After the landing he was asked to look at his hands, and he saw with surprise and pleasure that both beakers were still in perfect condition. This success had taken quite a bit of effort on Harry's part, and he was enormously satisfied, as his hands were not perspiring at all. Moreover, he was completely free of muscle pain, and realized for the first time that even landing can be carefree!

If you recognize that you have similar habits to Harry, try to become aware of them and carry out the following exercise in your imagination, over several days before the flight. Concentrate on imaginary plastic cups in your hands, which have to remain undamaged during take-off and landing. It will make your take-off completely different from the way you behaved using your old habits. You will hardly notice what is going on around you, and surprisingly quickly you, safely ensconced inside your plane, will leave the ground. Maybe you will not notice the time passing, until well after the take-off, when the undercarriage has already been retracted. This exercise is, however, no guarantee for the rest of the flight. Just try it in reality, like Harry. Before take-off and landing, hold a plastic cup in each hand, and monitor your progress. We hope it will encourage you to practise it more often, until you scarcely notice that the aircraft is already taxiing back to the gate.

People such as Mary and Harry frequently tormented themselves at certain moments of the flight by constantly repeating a phrase that inspired fear. By being given another task to concentrate on, this produced spectacular results. The method is very simple, but it requires a deliberate effort by the person concerned. You first have to be aware that at certain moments a certain phrase is running through your head, making you more and more anxious and tense. By deliberately concentrating on a useful activity, you avoid feeding the negative emotions, and the tense moments pass more easily.

I hope that the above examples make it clear how these techniques can help you, too.

If you are tense and worried, it is difficult not to think about your worries, but clinging on to these thoughts makes you feel even worse, and before you know it you are caught in a vicious circle of fear. If you permit yourself the luxury of not paying attention to the symptoms, you will find that they go away all by themselves, particularly if you concentrate on something else instead.

109

Thought retraining

Cognitive behaviour therapy (CBT) was developed from extensive research. It was found that people did more than respond to rewards and punishments. Their behaviour and emotions depended to a large extent on what they understood was happening. What people think and anticipate can greatly affect their reaction to events and people. CBT looks at the relationship between what people think, say, and do. The Greek philosopher Epictetus stated, 'People are disturbed not by things, but by the views which they take of them.' CBT has been used successfully to treat many different types of problems, particularly anxiety and depression. Having understood what one is thinking, and seen how this affects one's feelings and behaviour, it can often be possible to train oneself in a different way. The new behaviour can then lead to a potentially more satisfying way of life and become part of the person's normal pattern of existence.

We now turn to look specifically at your ideas about flying. These may not always be realistic, so it is a good idea to evaluate them. Try to consider whether your ideas about flying agree with reality, or whether they are emotionally coloured and actually untrue. Are your ideas likely to be helpful for you to overcome your fear of flying, or are they the opposite?

Every nervous flyer has different ideas about flying, so the following are only examples.

Suppose you are obsessed with the thought that flying in turbulence is dangerous. Try saying to yourself, 'Hold it right there!' Remind yourself that this is untrue; and that flying in turbulence is not dangerous. If you do not change your ideas, you will inevitably be afraid, and you will not achieve your objective of carefree flying. Try to encourage realistic thoughts. Remind yourself that air is to an aircraft as water is to a boat, or as the road is to a car. Tell yourself that an aircraft is designed to be strong yet flexible, so it can stand up to shocks, just like a boat can stand up to waves, and a car can stand up to bumps in the road. Repeat these things to yourself.

Go over all your ideas about flying, one by one. If any of them turn out to be unrealistic, replace them with accurate ones. Use the information in the earlier chapters. When you come across a misconception, tell yourself, 'Hold it right there', and think of the accurate information with which to replace it. Try to correct misconceptions. It is a good idea to do this out loud, at least when you first begin. The aim is to become aware of the inaccuracies and unrealistic thinking in your ideas about flying. This will lead to a more realistic, and hence more positive, attitude towards air travel. If you have other anxious thoughts – and you surely will, since it is not possible to cover all irrational thoughts in this book – you should try to think of positive alternatives, either by yourself or with the help of others. Write down these alternatives, and repeat them to yourself.

Discovering what you think is easier said than done. In particular, the types of thoughts that make you feel worse are often difficult to recognize. Frequently they are automatic thoughts, arising unbidden, and no sooner have they come then they are gone again. They are like bad habits. You may not even be conscious of them, because you are so used to them.

On the following pages you will find four common examples of thoughts that make people afraid before and during a flight (1(A), 2(A), 3(A), 4(A)). For each thought,

111

an alternative is given – a new thought that may help you to feel less anxious or even free of fear (1(B), 2(B), 3(B), 4(B)).

1(A) 'I can't get out of here and I should always be able to get out of every situation as soon as I want to! I've always got to have a way out, otherwise I get panicky.'

1(B) It is true that you cannot get out of a plane once in the air, but what you really mean is, 'I don't believe that it's possible for me to feel calm and relaxed if I'm sitting in an enclosed space like this cabin, where I can't wander in and out.' These thoughts only increase your fear. As long as you keep telling yourself, 'I've got to get out' when the door is locked, then of course you are making yourself more nervous, because there is something about the situation (a locked door) that you tell yourself should not be so. So instead of telling yourself, 'I can't get out of here, but I should be able to', help yourself by saying, 'True, I can't get out of here, but how can I make things as pleasant and comfortable as possible for myself? There's no good reason for why I need to get out! I can breathe normally because the air is replaced entirely every three minutes. Given that there is sufficient oxygen, I can work on making my breathing as normal as I can.'

2(A) 'Something's bound to go wrong!'

2(B) You can answer this by asking yourself what evidence you have that something is BOUND to go wrong. Everything could, and in fact is much more likely to, go according to plan. Both alternatives are possible, but experience shows that that the latter scenario is much, much, more probable and realistic than the former. In other words, by asking myself 'What if something goes wrong?' and forgetting the much more probable alternative, I am simply sending my thoughts in the wrong direction, and making myself more anxious as a result. In fact, I am behaving as if the 'going wrong' scenario is more probable than the 'going right' one, and that is pretty unreasonable.

If I want to improve things for myself and make things as pleasant as possible, it would be better to say, 'Of course, nobody knows how a flight is going to end, but if we look at it logically, the chances of everything going normally are much, much greater than the opposite possibility.'

Instead of getting fixated on an extremely improbable event, I should answer these thoughts, and then concentrate on things that can make the flight pleasant and enjoyable for me.

In practical terms, that can mean focusing my attention on things that can give me a certain amount of pleasure, such as reading a book, talking to people, watching the film, and other activities like this. Each time I catch myself saying, 'Something's bound to go wrong!', I must say, 'Wait a moment', and then answer the particular fear, and then start to concentrate on something else.

3(A) 'I have to keep watching everything that happens. What's going on here? This situation is dangerous, perhaps extremely dangerous. If I can only keep my eye on everything, perhaps nothing awful will happen.'

3(B) Is this really true? Do I really have to note everything that goes on around me: the noise of the engines, the sound of the landing gear, the way the flight attendants walk up and down the aisle, the way they look at the people, whether the Fasten seatbelts sign is on?

Of course, the answer is 'No', I don't have to notice every little thing. That's the pilot's job! In fact, it is much better to concentrate on something more useful. If I keep up the impossible attempt to notice every little thing, it is because I am suspicious, it is because I am obsessed by an insidious thought. The world does not obey our thoughts. No matter how intensely I observe, it does not help one little bit. And in any case, it is not possible to see on the faces of the flight attendants if something serious is happening. The truth is, I am continually on the lookout for information which it is impossible to obtain, and by doing so I just make myself nervous and anxious. I am only making things difficult and unpleasant for myself, both for my mind and my body.

The reality is I do not have to keep observing at all. In fact, it is much better not to keep watching everything. Instead, I should tell myself, 'I must try and concentrate on something more useful. Watching doesn't help. It cannot prevent anything. The chance of anything happening is extremely small. As long as I am sitting on a plane and have to choose between making myself tense and nervous or enjoying myself, I should choose the latter, and make things as pleasant for myself as possible.' Of course, I cannot help noticing something now and then that makes me anxious, but then I should simply tell myself, 'OK, I've started watching out again, but now I have to stop. I am going to concentrate on more enjoyable, useful, nicer or more interesting things.'

4(A) 'I can't be so tense without good reason – there must be something wrong, something is going happen to me.'

4(B) How can you be sure that something is going to happen to you? Of course you feel frightened if you imagine that you are going to be involved in an air disaster. But just because you are feeling frightened, does this mean you will therefore be involved in a disaster? This is obviously a non sequitur. Many people imagine that if they feel tense, it means there must be some external threat, some lurking danger. This assumes that they can tell from their feelings what is going around them. It would be wonderful if we had this kind of magical power, but unfortunately the reality is different.

We can feel tense for all sorts of imaginary reasons, while in actual fact there is not the remotest danger.

What you really should say to yourself is, 'It's only natural for me to be a little nervous, but that's all there is to it. I just have to decide not to make the tension any worse. Instead, I should use the tension to concentrate on other things, things that will make the flight as pleasant and enjoyable for me as possible.' Whenever I catch myself focusing on my own tension and making it worse as a result, I should tell myself, 'This tension is purely self-made. It does not mean that some sort of danger is lying in wait for me. What it does mean is that I should divert myself from these worrying thoughts, and that's just what I'm going to do, by reading my book, watching the film, looking out of the window, talking, or eating – but preferably not all at once!'

Relaxation and breathing exercises

A simple breathing exercise

You should do the exercises at a point in your day when you have some time for yourself and are not in a rush. Make yourself comfortable: find a nice, comfy chair, one that supports the whole body, including the head. Do not

115

slump: sit up straight with your back against the back of the chair and your feet directly below your knees, flat on the floor. Rest your arms on the arms of the chair or on the upper part of your legs. You can also start by doing the exercise in bed, but then you run the risk of falling asleep, which is not the intention here. If you do practise initially lying down, once you are familiar with the exercise, it is better to move from the bed to a chair.

Close your eyes and place a hand – preferably your dominant hand – on your abdomen (lower tummy), just under your navel. When you breathe in, this hand will rise up slightly due to the movement of the diaphragm. When you breathe out, the hand falls once more. Calmly keep your attention on this up and downward movement of your hand. This is all there is to it! You can also do this exercise in a sitting position.

An ideal time for practising this exercise is just before your flight. You can easily do it in the departure hall, the waiting area, or at home before your flight. You may wonder just how this 'low breathing' can help. By consciously switching back to a low breathing at certain times, you can reduce the intensity of your emotional reaction and so deal better with any particular situation.

To reduce your anxiety and tension while flying, do the following breathing exercise. This exercise is designed to make your breathing more regular. Sit up straight in your plane seat and start to breathe in through your nose while counting, 'One thousand and one, one thousand and two, one thousand and three.' Expand your diaphragm and tummy while counting.

Hold your breath and count once more, 'One thousand and one, one thousand and two, one thousand and three.' Open your mouth while breathing out as slowly as possible, but let all the air go, once again repeating the count.

Before you inhale again, hold your breath for three seconds and count, 'One thousand and one, one thousand and two, one thousand and three.' Then breathe in again through your nose, making sure your tummy expands at the navel while you count again, 'One thousand and one, one thousand and two, one thousand and three.'

Hold your breath and count, 'One thousand and one, one thousand and two, one thousand and three.' Open your mouth while you breathe out, once again repeating the count.

Wait and remain sitting calmly without breathing, and count, 'One thousand and one, one thousand and two, one thousand and three.' Repeat this exercise about ten times, but for at least three minutes.

Once you have completed the exercise, you are likely to find that your rate of breathing is slower and calmer. It is important to also employ the techniques of dealing with the anxious thoughts that we have described. Be aware of your behaviour, and also how both muscle tension and avoidance behaviour can make things more difficult for you.

If you congratulate yourself on not allowing yourself to go into the 'panic spiral' that you used to experience, and then allow yourself to move on to something interesting and absorbing – perhaps thinking or talking about all the wonderful things you plan to do when you reach your destination – the whole journey is likely to pass in a very different fashion from the way it did before you mastered your new skills. When you do notice that you have calmed down, congratulate yourself on your new ability to deal with your previous problem!

Relaxation exercises – going deeper

Sit or lie down comfortably and make yourself as relaxed as you can. Feel the support of the bed or chair under your body. Concentrate on your breathing . . . try to breathe easily and calmly . . . breathe slowly in . . . hold your breath in for two or three seconds . . . and then breathe out completely, while relaxing all your muscles.

We are going to do this again, but this time noting the difference between tension and relaxation. While you breathe in, tense your thigh muscles . . . curl your toes and feet upwards . . . clench your fists . . . stretch your arms and neck . . . place your chin on your chest . . . tense the muscles of your face . . . tense the muscles of your chest, abdomen, and back. Breathe in . . . hold your breath for three seconds and maintain the muscle tension . . . breathe out slowly and calmly . . . and let the tension flow away. . . all your muscles gradually become relaxed . . . feel the tension disappear from all the muscles.

Repeat the exercise once more. Make sure you take deep, abdominal breaths. Tense all your muscles once more . . . feel the tension . . . hold your breath in and maintain the tension . . . and while you calmly breathe out, let all your muscles slowly relax once more. Let your breathing proceed naturally . . . calm, even, and relaxed. While thinking of the word 'relax', gently close your eyes in order to experience even greater relaxation.

Now let us focus on particular muscle groups.

Concentrate on your left foot . . . let the muscles in your left foot go loose, loose and completely relaxed . . . let the relaxation spread to your lower part of your left leg, and then the upper part . . . let the muscles go loose and completely relaxed. Do the same with the right foot . . .

let the muscles in your right foot go loose, loose and completely relaxed . . . let the relaxation spread to the lower part of your right leg, and then the upper part. Both your left and right leg are now loose, loose and completely relaxed. Your legs are loose and heavy – heavy because they are being pulled down by gravity. Let the relaxation spread to your thighs and hips . . . release the muscles there too, and let the tension disappear . . . Let the relaxation go further, to your lower back . . . and to your tummy. Relax the back muscles and the tummy muscles . . . completely loose, loose and relaxed . . . let all the tension disappear.

Concentrate on your stomach. Relax the muscles there too . . . note how each time you breathe out, your whole body becomes more and more relaxed. Let the relaxation spread to your chest . . . let the muscles in your chest go loose, loose and completely relaxed . . . the shoulder muscles too go loose and completely relaxed.

Concentrate on your right arm . . . let your right arm go loose and completely relaxed . . . upper arm and lower arm, right down to the fingertips. Concentrate on your left arm . . . let your left arm go loose and completely relaxed . . . upper arm and lower arm . . . right down to the fingertips. Let the arms lie loose and relaxed.

Your whole trunk, your arms and legs are loose, loose and relaxed . . . wonderfully loose and limp and floppy, just like a rag doll. Now concentrate on your throat and neck . . . let the tension disappear from your throat . . . and let go of the tension in the neck muscles.

Let the relaxation spread to your head . . . relax the muscles in your face . . . the muscles of your forehead . . . let the tension flow out of the forehead muscles . . . keep your eyes gently closed . . . and let a heavy feeling come over your eyelids . . . a feeling as if you don't have any desire to open your eyes. Relax the jaws too . . . let the tension disappear from your lips and mouth . . . try to let go of all the tension in your face . . . all the face muscles go loose, loose and completely relaxed.

All the muscles in your body are now completely loose, loose and completely relaxed. Note how each time you breathe out, you become even more deeply relaxed . . . more and more loose, loose and relaxed . . . feel how wonderful it is to be so comfortable and at ease.

If you still feel tension left somewhere in your body, take a deep breath in . . . and concentrate on the spot where you still feel the tension . . . then breathe out again gently . . . and let the tension disappear from there too.

Enjoy the rest and relaxation you have given yourself in this way . . . enjoy the pleasant feeling, and think of enjoyable events . . . take plenty of time . . . and remain relaxed just as long as you want.

When you want to finish the exercise, count slowly down from five to one . . . while gently breathing in . . . open your eyes . . . and slowly tense some of your muscles. The more you move about, the fresher and more restful you will start to feel.

After doing this exercise a few times, you will notice that you are able to relax more quickly and easily, and that it makes you feel good. If it doesn't work the first time, don't give up hope immediately. It may be difficult to begin with, but you will eventually learn to relax. If, on the other hand, you have mastered the relaxation exercises and feel comfortable, then you can go on to the next step. In the meantime, it is useful to note how often you tend to tense your muscles unnecessarily in the course of a day: how often you clench your fists, clutch the arm of your chair, clench your jaws or hunch your shoulders. Whenever you notice yourself tensing in this way, try to relax and concentrate on your breathing.

Putting it all together

Think of situations to do with flying, in which you feel fear. Make a list of ten to fifteen situations, and draw them up in order. Put the situations in which you are least afraid at the top, followed by others in increasing order of scariness. At the bottom of the list are those situations of which you are totally terrified.

Each person's list will, of course, be different. The following example might fit someone who is most scared of flying in turbulent weather:

1. I'm at home and I think of airports and aircraft.
2. I'm driving along the road and I see a plane take off.
3. I've decided to travel by air, and have bought the tickets.
4. I'm on my way to the airport in order to catch a flight.
5. I'm in the departures hall, I've checked in, and now I'm waiting for my flight number to be called.
6. I step on board the plane, sit in my seat and fasten my safety belt.
7. I'm sitting in a plane with the doors closed, ready to take off.
8. I'm sitting in a plane flying at cruising height in calm weather.
9. I'm sitting in a plane that's about to land.
10. I'm sitting in a plane climbing up to cruising altitude.

11. I'm sitting in a plane, and look down out of the window.
12. I'm sitting in a plane as it accelerates for take-off and leaves the ground.
13. I'm sitting in a plane, when a warning signal sounds and the 'Fasten Seatbelts' sign comes on.
14. I'm sitting in a plane flying at cruising height, when the captain announces that turbulence is expected.
15. I'm sitting in a plane that's bumping about as it flies through turbulence.

The idea is for you to draw up your own list.

1. ....
2. ....
3. ....
4. ....
5. ....
6. ....
7. ....
8. ....
9. ....
10. ....
11. ....
12. ....
13. ....
14. ....
15. ....

If you have trouble flying because in an aircraft it feels as if you are trapped in a small, enclosed space, then you probably also have difficulty with other enclosed spaces. In such a case, your list can concentrate on this aspect.

Start with an enclosed space in which you are only slightly uncomfortable, and end with the dreaded aircraft, where every seat is occupied! On the way, you can take in a wide-bodied jet, such as a Boeing 747 or Airbus A340, and narrow it down to the smaller, more cramped, packed plane, carrying you to the final destination.

Perhaps it is not the flying that bothers you, but rather that you do not dare to look out of the window. Number one on the list might then be a glimpse of the window, item two a longer look, and the final item a long, panoramic view of the ground below, where you are fully aware of height.

If you cannot bring yourself to get out of your seat on an aircraft, for instance in order to go to the toilet, then start your list with small movements that you make in your seat, followed by standing up briefly and sitting down once more, then going to the toilet just to wash your hands, even keeping the door open, and so on.

Perhaps you have a fear of driving past an airport. If so, begin your list with driving along a road five miles from the airport. Item two is driving closer the airport, item three is driving right beside it, and so on, step by step.

Another example might be someone who would like to visit New York, but cannot because they are afraid of flying over water. If your situation is similar, your list could begin with short hops such as London to Paris, and then London–Amsterdam, then London–Oslo, and so on. These steps involve making such trips over longer and longer stretches of water, with the final step being the flight to New York.

Although every list will be different, they all start with a situation that can be faced relatively easily, and end with the most difficult situation. The situations in the list do not have to be in the chronological order in which they occur.

Don't be too ambitious with the first item; it should be just the first step towards the goal that you wish to attain. The steps between successive items should not be too large, either. If they are, insert extra steps between them. There can be as many steps as you want. However, it is important to be honest about what you fear. You also have to be capable of imagining yourself in these situations. If you have difficulty in this, try using illustrations or photographs to help you. You can take photographs yourself at the airport or in an aviation museum. It is also possible to borrow recordings of aircraft noises from public libraries.

Go through each point on your list, and consider your thoughts when you are in the situation – ask yourself whether your ideas agree with reality. For each situation, ask yourself:

1. Are my conceptions of this situation realistic, i.e. are they based on reality?
2. Do they help me achieve my chosen goal, namely to make a relaxed and pleasant trip by air?
3. Do they help me avoid upsetting tension and unpleasant feelings?

If the answer to any of these questions is 'no', then find the ideas that do match reality – if necessary referring to the earlier chapters – and write them down.

Next, begin your relaxation exercises, and continue until you are completely calm and relaxed.

Once you are relaxed, imagine yourself in the first situation on your list. Try to maintain the picture for five minutes, while remaining relaxed. While you are doing this, try to maintain correct, realistic thoughts about the situation. If you feel tension mounting, let go of all your thoughts and concentrate on relaxing once more. When you are calm and relaxed once more, then start again.

Once you can experience the situation three times in your imagination, for five minutes each time, without anxiety or tension, then you can go on to the next item on your list. If you do not manage to relax in this next situation, then the step may be too big. In that case, think of a situation between the two. Once you can imagine that three times for five minutes and remain relaxed, make another attempt at the situation you couldn't manage. Go through the whole list in this way.

Once it all goes well as an armchair exercise, it is time to start practising the situations for real. This means, for example, actually driving near an airport. Try this several times, each time going one stage further. For example, you can obtain actual travel guides and look through them.

If you are able to fly, but cannot relax because you do not dare go to the toilet, you can practise that. Begin by getting out of your seat and going to the rear of the aircraft, then go inside the toilet and wash your hands, and so on. You will find that it goes better each time: the more you practise, the easier it gets. Make sure you stay relaxed and breathe easily. Go a step further each time, just as you did in your imagination. If you feel tension rising, do the relaxation exercise until you are calm once more. Note, however, that not everything you feel is necessarily 'tension'. It may simply be excitement, and a certain amount of excitement is perfectly natural when travelling, so you should just let yourself try to accept it.

At this point you may be wondering how such a method works. The answer lies in the power of imagination. If you can remain calm when you picture yourself in a certain situation, then it is possible that you can do it in real life as well. When dealing with fears and how to overcome them, imagination is the next best thing to the real world.

Finally, it is important to learn how to apply the exercises even if you are frightened or tense.

Once you have learned to relax in calm situations, you can apply what you have learned to flying and coping with the situation in an aircraft. Whether standing or sitting, you should adopt a relaxed posture. Don't sit on the edge of your airline seat, and try not to hunch your shoulders or clench your fists. Being tense can be very tiring, so you should not waste energy by maintaining an uncomfortable posture. Allow your body some rest and relaxation, even when you are doing something. For example, try to relax when you are eating, or when you are queuing to check in.

You are ready for this when you know which parts of your body suffer most from tension. The relaxation will work better if you concentrate on these parts. Practise the relaxation exercises on the previous pages.

A quick version of this is to try the following:

1. Let your shoulders drop.
2. Relax the most tense part of your body, for instance your hands.
3. Breathe slowly and evenly.
4. Repeat a phrase to yourself such as, 'Just let the tension go.'
5. Enjoy the new feeling, and then choose another part of your body to relax, if you want to.

Check to see if you are tense whenever you think of flying, and do the above exercises in order to relax.

One final, simple breathing exercise that you can carry out in situations you have found difficult is to continue to breathe calmly by placing your right hand on your lower abdomen and breathing in through your nose. Say 'ten' in your head, and breathe out through your mouth. Take another breath in through your nose, say 'nine', and breathe out again through your mouth. Carry on in this way, counting down to zero. This simple breathing exercise can actually alleviate all sorts of physical stress reactions. The heart beats more gently, and the risk of anger, fear, or panic reactions diminishes.

Just bear in mind that it takes time before you learn to relax quickly. Give yourself a chance, and don't expect results too quickly

Handy hints

If you are 'struggling' with this book, let someone who is able to fly read it and then talk it through with you. Don't give up on it.

1. Visit airports. Somewhere on the perimeter of all airports is a vantage point from where you can watch the planes take off and land. Observe the different makes and sizes. Find out which you will be travelling on and learn to recognize it.
2. If you have reason to be concerned about your physical health, speak to your doctor regarding whether there are any medical reasons why you should not fly.
3. Once you have been reassured of your physical health, then remind yourself that a panic attack can give rise

to increased arousal – the 'fight or flight' response. As you now know, this is a sudden onset of intense fear or discomfort, associated with an increase in rate of breathing, breathlessness, sweating, palpitations, trembling, and giddiness. You may also notice tingling of the face and limbs, light-headedness, muscle spasms, nausea, hot or cold feelings, blurred vision, and faintness. Try to move away from concentrating on how you are feeling, and concentrate on other things, as concentration on the feelings tends to make them grow stronger. Remind yourself that panic symptoms are normal physical sensations: they are not dangerous for either your body or your mind.

4. Select a destination that is particularly meaningful to you. If you have friends there, anticipate being with them.

5. Consider bringing someone with you who is familiar with your problem and who is caring and understanding. Don't give in to the impulse to turn and flee. Handle just one minute at a time

6. Expect to be nervous, excited, and uneasy. Accept all these feelings. Big events like this have always given you similar feelings. Leaving home, starting a new job, getting married, being stopped by a policeman – all give you mixed feelings. Accept what is happening to you, and do not try to avoid it. If you just 'hang on in there', you'll find that the fear starts to go away.

7. Make sure you pack in plenty of time. Choose comfortable clothes that fit easily. Take into account the weather at your destination.

8. If you know that you usually have problems with travel sickness, take medication, if necessary, to deal with it.

It is helpful to concentrate on the view of horizon, so try to choose a window seat. This can reduce feelings of nausea. It is particularly important to have a meal, so that you don't fly on an empty stomach. Make sure you have your prescribed medication with you.

9. Leave for the airport in plenty of time, so you do not have to rush. Take delays into account, and be early. Give yourself extra time for parking, walking, even having a cup of coffee or tea, checking in, choosing a seat at your leisure, and going through security screening. Rushing will only add to your anxiety.

10. Always eat a meal before flying, avoid alcohol, and drinks containing caffeine.

11. When travelling, concentrate on what is going on around you. Do not try to pretend that you are not at an airport, or that you are not on a plane. Rather, look around and pay attention to your surroundings. Be careful not to misinterpret information, however.

12. Try not to withdraw into your shell, but get involved in something specific. Talk to the people sitting next to you, write to someone, or prepare your work. Behave as you would if you were seated in other situations. Concentrate on what you are doing, and if you do have any negative thoughts, argue with them, using the skills you have learnt. Practise reframing any negative thoughts about the situation, reminding yourself of the logical facts. Go over the actual characteristics of the situation in your mind. In this way, you can move on from the frightening thoughts that could otherwise exacerbate your panic if you do not deal with them. Think about the pleasant things you are going to do at your destination.

13. Buy a magazine or a book to entertain you. Perhaps something quite gripping, maybe with pictures! Being occupied is preferable to fear.

14. If possible, to be more comfortable, ask for a seat near the front where it is quieter or smoother.

15. Make sure your breathing remains calm.

16. Look around you at each different step of the proceedings. Don't concentrate on how you are feeling, but rather try to focus on the building, the people, the cabin, and the activity around you.

17. If you find yourself thinking of why you won't succeed, give at least equal time to considering the reasons why you can succeed, and why you need to.

18. Breathing can be a primary antidote to fear. Try to keep your breathing slow and deep, as if you were just relaxing. Moving about can help considerably. Move your feet, shift about on your seat, move your arms, hands, and fingers. Do not sit rigid, as this increases the fear.

19. As you come on board, tell the cabin crew that you are a bit nervous. The crew will be friendly, but recognize that it is often difficult for them to understand how anyone can be afraid. To them it is like travelling by car, bus, or train. Some crew, however, have had extra training in understanding people who are afraid of flying.

20. When you sit down, talk to other passengers. However, don't talk incessantly, because that is a common way to avoid your feelings. Those feelings are all right, but it is unhelpful to deny or repress them. Don't focus on them to the exclusion of your surroundings.

21. Make yourself comfortable. Loosen your shoes, or even take them off. Make sure your clothing is not too tight.

22. Pay calm attention to the standard safety briefing given by the flight attendants.

23. Even seated and belted, there is still a lot of body movement you can do. Do it! It is so important. Act more than react. Yawn, smile at a baby, watch the safety demonstration, remembering that these are precautions for your own safety. Remind yourself that the crew would not be doing this job if it were as dangerous as you may fear.

24. Breathe deeply as the plane lines up for take-off. Lean back in your seat. Keep your eyes open, and look out of the window. Do not grip on to anything. Wiggle your toes, faster and faster as the plane accelerates. Take-off usually only takes 25–65 seconds, depending on the type of the plane and the temperature of the air outside. Be aware that if it takes longer, this is not necessarily a signal that there is anything amiss.

25. After take-off, recognize the sounds such as the landing gear being retracted, or the intermittent sound of the flaps being retracted. Remind yourself that *you* do not have to know what every sound means – that's the Captain's job!

26. Try eat and even enjoy the food on board. Avoid high-protein food, especially on long flights, as this will help you to sleep more easily. It is best to eat carbohydrates, such as pasta, or spaghetti without meat, as this will help your body to prepare for rest periods. Drink more fluids than you usually do, such as water, lemonade, fruit juice, or milk, because the air on board is fairly dry.

131

27. If you hear, feel, or see something that you do not understand and want to know what it is, look it up in the 'Knowledge is Power' section in this book.

28. Look around you, look outside, go with the movement of the plane. Don't anticipate or resist it. You are part of it now. If you still feel uncomfortable or tense, wiggle your bottom, your legs or arms. Conduct your favourite piece of music. If you run into turbulent weather, remember that the aircraft can deal with it easily. Remember that everyone can bear it, and so can you, too. Just imagine you are driving over a bumpy road, or that you are in a boat going up and down with the waves. Don't try to resist the movement: just go with it, and let yourself be rocked along with and within the plane.

29. Eat the meal, watch the film, read your book, but remember, not all at the same time! Try to really concentrate on whichever activity you are doing.

30. As soon as you are permitted, stand up, and stretch, move about, rejoice. You 'have slipped the surly bonds of earth'. As one former fearful flyer put it, 'The lion that once roared at me, turned out to be a pussycat.' Congratulate yourself. Remember, in the words of the Buddha, 'The greatest victory of all is the victory over one's self.'

31. If you have had a good, enjoyable flight, promise yourself to take another trip by air soon. You will find that it is even easier and more pleasant the next time, especially if you keep applying what you have learnt at moments when you feel frightened.

32. Learn to appreciate compliments from friends, family, or business relations for having flown. This will increase your pleasure, give you courage, and build up

your self-confidence. Give yourself compliments for having so bravely faced your fear. Remember that:

Brave

To be brave is to behave
bravely when your heart is faint.
So you can be really brave
only when you really ain't.

Piet Heiu Grooks.

CHAPTER FOUR

LAST, BUT NOT LEAST

Travel companions: dos and don'ts

This section deals with ways in which a travelling companion can help another passenger who is afraid of flying.

'Don't Think About It!'; 'Pull Yourself Together!'; 'There's Nothing to be Scared Of!'; 'You'll be All Right!'; 'It's All in Your Mind!'; 'Don't Be So Silly!'

These commonly employed exhortations are probably some of the most UNHELPFUL things that one person can say to another, even when said for the very best of intentions. They give no idea as to what the person with the problem can actually DO, and usually serve to damage further the already shaky self-confidence and self-esteem.

Many people say the very same thing to themselves when they feel uneasy or anxious. The problem is that a feeling does not go away or diminish just because we deny or condemn it. Just as a painful wound is not cured by not treating it, a painful feeling is not cured by simply ignoring it, or telling it to go away. Rule number one for a healthy relationship is to make it clear to the other person that you are trying to understand how they feel.

Consider this scenario. The weather has been arctic, the wind blowing the snow along fiercely. There has been some doubt as to whether or not the flight will be cancelled. Finally, the announcement to board is given. During the safety briefing, it is mentioned that under the circumstances passengers are advised to remain in their seats, and to keep their seatbelts fastened at all times. While one person may interpret this as a safety precaution, the other can start to panic, and begin suggesting that perhaps it is best to leave now. Rather than resorting to the totally counterproductive, oft-employed phrases displayed above, it would be far more helpful for the non-fearful person to say something along the lines of, 'I can quite understand how that scares you now', and then to help the frightened person start looking at the reasons why it is likely to be safe to fly on that day, reminding them also of the positive reasons why they are taking that particular trip.

The second rule is closely related to the first. Even if you cannot do anything about what is causing the fear in the other person, you can usually do something to help them bear it more easily, or, at the very least, prevent it from becoming worse. You can do this by lending support in the form of:

- talking to the other person about their fear, instead of trying to dismiss it;
- offering sympathy or physical comfort.

Let's face it, deep down, adults are just big kids in many ways. If a child is frightened or tearful, it can usually be soothed by hugging, stroking, or comforting in some other way. The same can apply equally well to adults. One of the most impressive demonstrations of this comes from research in which patients in a hospital were visited by the surgeon on the day before their operation. In those cases where the surgeon touched the patient now and then during the discussion about the operation, laying his or her hand on the patient's arm for a moment, for instance, the patient not only appeared to be less anxious, but also did better after the surgery. The same applies to everyday situations. By saying to your companion, 'If we start to get buffeted about and you get scared, then just hang on to me, or let me hold you', you help them to resist their fear, instead of trying and failing to resist the fact that they are afraid.

Unfortunately, there are too many adults, who think, 'No way am I going to make a fool of myself in front of everybody by going all soppy and hanging round her/his neck.' But perhaps it is better to tell yourself that you are not likely to lose face in front of people you do not care about, and to remind yourself that, above all, you do not want to compromise your relationship with someone you do care about.

Eight top tips for travelling companions

1. Take the fear seriously. Above all, don't dismiss it.
2. If you yourself become frightened, admit it honestly. The other person will then understand that their reaction is not so disproportionate after all, and they will see that you feel normal once more, after your moment of fear.
3. Pay attention to the other person. Don't abandon them, even if they seem to be putting up a barrier. Try to prevent your companion from withdrawing into him or her self.

4. Let the other person talk, and show that you understand their fear.

5. Offer something to drink, preferably water, milk, or a soft drink, but not coffee, tea, or alcohol.

6. Talk about something that interests the other person. For example, what the two of you are going to do when you arrive, or something entertaining that the other person has done recently.

7. If you can be tactful about it, point out to the other person which group of muscles they are tensing, and how this is not helpful for them. You might offer to do a breathing or relaxation exercise from this book with them.

8. You can also help the other person to feel better about flying by giving them compliments, and encouraging friends and family to do the same once the nervous flyer has actually flown. This gives the sufferer more courage for the next time, and builds up their self-confidence.

Frequently asked questions

'What's it like way up there?' is quite a normal question when you have never flown, or when you have never dared to look out of the window. Frequent flyers and pilots will tell you that it can be really beautiful! Sunsets and sunrises are spectacular. It would be great if everyone could learn to look at it this way. At 35,000 feet above our planet, the air is clear and smooth. The far horizon is a long way off. From the vantage point of 35,000 feet up, the line of sight distance to the far horizon is 250 miles. The temperature in the cabin is in the low twenties centigrade (seventies

Fahrenheit), but outside that window it is −60° C (−55° F), i.e., below zero. That cold outside air is compressed by the big jet engines to pressurize your cabin to a comfortable level of about 6,500 feet. You are travelling close to 500 miles an hour, but unless the plane is accelerating or decelerating, you do not have any awareness of movement.

If you have never flown, or if you last flew a long time ago, it is understandable that that there are a lot of questions running through your mind. It can be a fear of the unknown.

However, fear of flying is not necessarily just a fear of the unknown but, as has been shown, it also can be summed up as a fear of a 'loss of control' – either internal or external. As previously explained, these fears encompass others such as the fear of being closed in (claustrophobia), heights, being out of control (either by giving up control to someone else, such as the pilot, or fear of losing control of oneself, perhaps 'going crazy', fainting, having a heart attack, or even dying).

We have therefore listed below twenty-six frequently asked questions that have been compiled from the many questions asked by people learning to overcome their fear of flying, and we deal with the most common misunderstandings about fear, anxiety, and about aviation.

1. How many people fly daily worldwide?
   On average, every twenty-four hours worldwide, more than twelve million people have been up in the air. In 2006, 235 million people used airports in the UK and there were two and a half million take-offs and landings just at UK airports alone (CAA, 2007).
2. I don't know anyone else with fear of flying. Are there others like me?

You are not the only one, there are many more. Published estimates indicate that one in every five adults is afraid of flying. Studies have indicated that 14% of the adult population has never flown due to psychological reasons, largely related to a fear of flying. It has also been estimated that one in four flyers shows a significant degree of fear or anxiety during parts of the flight.

3. Are more women afraid of flying than men, or are there other sex differences?

   No, at first sight it looks as if there are more women who are afraid of flying, but that is probably because woman are more likely to admit to their fear. There are also cultural differences. In the Far East it can be even more difficult for men to admit that they are afraid.

4. How dangerous is flying?

   Statistics tell us clearly that flying is the safest form of travel. There are interesting comparisons from the UK and the USA, such as: it is more than 100 times safer to fly than to drive; you are more likely to die in a horse riding accident than an aircraft accident; five fully laden jumbo jets would have to crash every day with no survivors to equal the number of road deaths; more people die on the roads every day than are killed in a year of airline accidents, and you are more likely to be killed by your spouse than to die in an aircraft accident! To reiterate, flying really is the safest form of public transport!

5. Why do statistics not convince me?

   The problem with statistics is that they show patterns of large groups, but cannot predict the individual's fate. Many people know the chances are extremely small, but still reply – 'I know it is only one in however many, as you say . . . but . . . who's going to be the one? A similar analogy can be used looking at statistics and the National Lottery. While you apparently have a greater chance of being dead by the end of the week than of winning, who would happily and hopefully put weekly bets on the former?

6. What is the difference between a fear and a phobia?
Fears are common to us all. Without fear we would not be able to survive this world. Fears make us cautious about doing things like petting a growling dog, or crossing the road in heavy traffic. Realistically, danger is present in those situations. A phobia is not a cautionary response to danger. A phobia makes you avoid non-dangerous situations, because they feel threatening to you. Boarding an aeroplane is not dangerous; in fact, it is a lot safer than many other normal things in life, but someone who is phobic will feel threatened, tearful, overwhelmed, or panicky. A vivid and runaway imagination, then, creates more fright and more feelings of helplessness. Retreat gives immediate relief, and future avoidances will follow.

7. How do people try to avoid fear?
Many people avoid their fear by not flying at all. They can also try to avoid feeling scared by taking alcohol or medication, gripping the arms of their seat until their knuckles turn white, closing their eyes, sitting rigidly, talking incessantly, or even being mute. They may try to compensate for the aircraft's movement, by leaning left in a right turn, for example. Some even try to defy gravity by sitting 'lightly' on their seats. This resistance creates an exhausting and miserable experience. The elements of avoidance are counterproductive, and

only reinforce the problem. Trying not to be afraid, ironically, makes you more afraid.

8. Owing to my job, I am not able to avoid flying, but the more I fly, the worse it gets. I thought that practice was supposed to make it better – remember the old adage 'practice makes perfect'?

   It all depends on what you are doing before and when you fly. If you are totally convinced that the next flight will be your last, and spend the time beforehand making your will and saying farewells, then this unpleasant lead-up will not put you in the best frame of mind before the journey. Likewise, if you spend the time away convinced that although you made it out, the return flight will be everything you fear, this anticipation will affect your feelings on the return flight. Practising the wrong thing just makes it worse! It is like practising the piano – but playing the wrong notes. No amount of practice can ever make the piece right. Therefore, you need to learn how to deal with the fear itself.

9. If alcohol and medication has not worked for me, is there still hope?

   As explained in Question Seven, alcohol and medication are forms of avoidance. They can be understood as working (or not) in the same way as taking painkillers for toothache, which may alleviate the pain, but not cure the problem. Specialists in the treatment of fear of flying regularly and successfully work with people who have tried and failed with many other approaches, including alcohol and medication. While medication can sometimes temporarily suppress the symptoms of fear of flying, you never build up your own self-confidence.

10. Is there no medication at all that can solve the problem? Medication only provides temporary relief. As such, it does have a use, but eventually it usually becomes less and less effective, requiring more and more to produce the same result. One serious disadvantage of medicines is that you can come to rely on them, and become dependent. Furthermore, why should you use medication to deal with something that you could learn to deal with on your own, and so build up your self-confidence in the process? Regular use of tranquillizers or anti-anxiety drugs usually makes it more difficult to build up self-confidence and belief in your own ability, because you never give yourself the chance to practise new habits or strategies. Furthermore, medication can frequently have side effects, making you, for instance, dizzy, drowsy, or absent-minded. Typical side effects are dryness of the mouth, eyes, and skin, and this can be worse in an aircraft where the air is already dry. As mentioned above, while medication can suppress fear symptoms, you never really overcome your fear of flying.

11. Can someone who is anxious for a longer period suffer physical consequences?

This is extremely unlikely for a normal, healthy person. It is important to realize that an increased heart rate that has been triggered by anxiety will not damage the heart. When you are anxious, your heart beats no faster than during sport or physical exercise, activities we often do for pleasure. Fear itself will not kill you. Your body is equipped to deal with natural fear reactions.

Heavy perspiration does not cause any harm. The same phenomenon happens when we take a sauna or sunbathe, activities that are done for relaxation. Fear does not cause any physical damage, although it may feel uncomfortable and unpleasant.

12. Can long-term anxiety lead to a nervous breakdown?
Fear is always an unpleasant emotion, but, as stated above, it cannot harm you physically. The unpleasant emotion disappears when the fear goes away, however long it may have lasted. While it can make you feel very tired, fear does not 'drive you mad' or make you 'mentally disturbed'. If you have had psychological problems in the past, it is always a good idea to discuss your difficulties with your doctor.

13. Could it be that my fear is inborn, so that I have to accept that it is just the way I am, and I cannot really do anything about it?
No. It is possible for some people to be more susceptible to fear and stress than others, but you can still learn to deal with the fear and stress better – sometimes much better – than you do now.

14. If I just leave the problem alone, and don't worry about it too much, will it go away on its own?
Sometimes. Problems of this nature can disappear with time. The only trouble is that it can take a very long time. If you learn to deal with the problem, you will get rid of it much quicker. Furthermore, by doing so you can learn strategies that can enable you to deal with other anxiety problems that arise in future, nipping them in the bud before they become a real nuisance.

15. Are thunderstorms and lightning dangerous?
Pilots avoid thunderstorms, by flying over or around them. The aircraft radar, and that used by the air traffic controllers on the ground, can easily determine the

size and intensity of the thunderstorms. The controllers are skilled professionals, and can clear the plane to another altitude or routing more comfortable to the passengers. Flying through a storm is very uncomfortable, but it is not dangerous. When flying in the vicinity of a thunderstorm, you will experience turbulence. If pilots have to fly through turbulence, they will slow down, as you would in your car on a rough road. Lightning is spectacular and awesome. However, the plane is a completely bonded metallic conductor and a lightning strike would not penetrate to the interior, or disable the aircraft. You are safe from lightning in the plane, both in the air and on the ground

16. What causes turbulence?

Turbulence is a word to describe any air that is not perfectly smooth. Choppiness is what is usually encountered in unstable air. Clear air turbulence (CAT) occurs at flight altitudes when two airstreams, travelling at different speeds, converge. The air is disturbed and choppy where they meet and blend. Imagine two fast-moving streams coming together to move on as a river. The plane rides the airwaves, just as a boat sails the sea. The surface can be choppy, but will not hurt the plane or you when you are wearing your safety belt. Air is always in motion. Even in a still room, smoke from a cigarette can be observed to waft and curl. Air in rapid motion becomes wind. An unsteady wind becomes gusty and unsteady when it moves across uneven terrain in the same way that water becomes choppy when it moves over a shallow rocky bed. So, if it is gusty as you drive to the airport, expect to experience some choppiness a few minutes after take-off as the wind gusts over the uneven terrain.

17. Circling in the clouds before landing makes me very nervous. Aren't we in danger of crashing?

    No. That circling is actually a holding pattern, precisely flown in a race-track-like shape, in designated areas within a few minutes access of the airport. The planes are 'stacked up' with a vertical separation of 1,000 feet and the plane's position is closely monitored on radar. When the plane at the bottom of the stack is cleared to approach and land, the others are individually and sequentially instructed to descend to an assigned altitude 1,000 feet below the altitude previously designated.

18. Do I need answers to all my questions and doubts about the planes, the air traffic control, airports, weather, before I feel relaxed?

    No, that is impossible. Fear of flying is not so much a problem about lack of knowledge regarding how planes work. It is usually because the person has difficulty handling the emotional and physical responses and reactions to flying, or to the thought of it. The person gets stuck in the 'What if' spiral, asking, 'What if one engine conks out on a four-engined plane?' Rather than being reassured with the answer that the plane can fly on three, the question is then put, 'What if the second engines fails?' Even when told that on just one engine, the pilot still has directional control, the person will go on to ask, 'What if all engines fail'. Giving the person information about the glide range still is unlikely to totally reassure them – there is always the next 'what if': for instance, that the nearest land is beyond the glide range, or there is no suitable landing strip. Treatment can teach ways of dealing with these 'What if' fears. Do not try to establish control of the outside world, control yourself by relaxing your body, and controlling your breathing and muscle tension.

19. What does the 'Ding-dong' signal in the cabin mean? When I hear it, I always think the worst.

    The 'Ding-dong' signal, most of the time, is triggered when passengers or other cabin crew call for cabin crew. Occasionally, the cockpit crew may sound the bell to signal that they want to talk to a member of the cabin crew. Each seat has a bell to call the cabin crew. Part of the fear on the plane can be caused by not knowing what is going on. An explanation from the captain as to why passengers should return to their seats, or why it has been necessary to abort the landing and make a second attempt, can enable the person to make sense of something that can otherwise be magnified considerably by their imagination. You can always ask the crew what a particular noise means, if you have never heard it before, but try not to do this for noises you have previously heard, as otherwise you could just start to go down the 'what if' spiral.

20. Why do planes fly so high?

    Height gives us several advantages; it is safer, faster, and cheaper. There is nothing to hit up there, and the height gives the pilots plenty of time to glide towards an airport or to solve a problem in the unlikely event that something went wrong with an engine. The air at 30,000 feet is less than half as dense as the air at 5,000 feet. The less dense or thinner air offers less resistance to our movement through it, and therefore

147

gives us more than twice the speed available at the lower altitude. We use less fuel up there too, because our fuel consumption decreases in direct proportion to the decrease in air density. Finally, and this is worth remembering, it is smoother high up above the clouds.

21. I am just awful from the moment the ticket is booked. The nearer the flight, the worse I get. Sometimes the flight is all right, but it is just not worth all that worry beforehand.

Very often, the anticipation is worse that the event. The anticipated fear of tomorrow can spoil today, if we let it. Play an active role at any moment you feel afraid, not only in the plane itself, but also at any time you find yourself anticipating something negative. Identify and argue with the thoughts, and then go on to do something else.

22. Watching the big planes land, they seem dangerously slow to me. Aren't they close to stalling?

No! The plane appears slow because of its immense size. A small executive jet at the same speed would appear to streak through the air twice as fast. Planes stay well above the stall speed. The speed maintained at all phases of the landing approach is at least 30% above the stall speed, based on a consideration of weight and the degrees of flap setting.

23. What sort of training do the pilots and cabin crew have?

All airline pilots, once fully qualified, are given training and competency checks every six months. No other profession is as closely examined, inspected, and monitored – except perhaps astronauts! Cabin crew also have to pass regular checks on their knowledge and performance. Their first and foremost responsibility is ensuring your safety. Before the Civil Aviation Authority allows any commercial jet to carry passengers, the plane's manufacturer has to show that a full load of passengers (up to 500 in the case of a Boeing 747, or up to 800 in an Airbus A380) can be evacuated completely in only ninety seconds, even with half the plane's exits blocked.

24. During the descent and landing, my eardrums sometimes bother me. While at times it is barely noticeable, at others it is painful. What can I do?

The discomfort is caused by the increase of atmospheric pressure against a sensitive eardrum as you descend. Modern aircraft are pressurized so that those changes are minimized. Chewing gum or sucking a sweet can help. Yawning is even better. It stretches the muscles that can open the pressure block in the Eustachian tube. If yawning and swallowing are not effective, the most forceful way to unblock your ears is to pinch your nostrils shut and take a mouthful of air. Then, using your cheek and throat muscles, force the air to the back of your nose as if you were trying to blow your thumb and fingers off your nostrils. When you hear a loud pop in your ears, you have unblocked them. You may have to repeat this several times during the descent. If you have a cold, take nose drops before the descent, or use earplugs, which are available at a pharmacy.

25. What happens if the Captain is unwell at a critical time like landing or take-off?

The aircraft is equipped with dual flight controls and duplicate flight instrumentation. Both pilot and co-pilot are equally qualified to fly the aeroplane. While one is landing, or taking off, the other is closely monitoring the procedure and could immediately take over if the need arose.

26. After reading this book, will I never worry about flying again?

   That is an unrealistic expectation. What you will be able to do is understand and deal with negative thought processes that develop. This can enable you to be in control of your emotions, and so you can learn to overcome your fear over time.

While every flight is different, we have covered the most frequently asked questions in this section. We trust that the information in this book will be sufficient to enable you to provide your own answers for any additional questions or uncertainties.

Professional assistance options

You have taken a very positive step by reading this book to this point, rather than just allowing your fear of flying to continue to dictate what you can and can't do in your life.

However, for some people, the self-help options, while improving matters somewhat, may not be sufficient to totally conquer their fear. If this is the case for you, you should not hesitate to seek support from those around you, or to get professional help, given that there are a number of very effective professional sources of assistance. Therapy for fear of flying is available from psychologists, psychiatrists, counsellors, and various 'alternative health' practitioners. Sometimes airlines offer courses. There are various therapy methods. The nature of the therapy is usually linked to the model of the cause that the therapists suggest is at the root of the fear. So, for those who believe in an unconscious cause, psychodynamic therapy would be the treatment of choice. However, long-term explorative psychoanalytic therapy has not been shown to be effective in the treatment of a fear of flying.

Treatments based on cognitive behavioural principles (CBT) have shown success in 70–98 per cent of people who sought help. Other treatments, such as systemic therapy, hypnosis, virtual reality, re-attributional training, systematic desensitization, stress inoculation training, coping self-talk, cognitive preparation, flooding, implosion, *in vivo* exposure, and relaxation training have all been used to treat fear of flying. In addition, there has also been work done with computer-assisted programmes. These use specific types of software that aims to confront people, in a hierarchically structured way, with real images and sounds related to the fear stimuli presented on the screen of a personal computer. Virtual Reality, an alternative computer-based technique, allows individuals to become active participants, interacting through sight, sound, and touch, in a computer-generated, three-dimensional world.

Most frequently, the treatment of choice for fear of flying is based on cognitive behavioural principles, given that these methods have been shown to be the most effective.

Delivery of treatment can be in various formats, from treating just one individual at a time to the partly individual, partly group method, or, alternatively, to treatment within a group of participants.

Professional help will often encompass many of the steps described in this book, including relaxation, which continues until the person can remain relaxed in the situation of which he or she was most frightened. Other features of professional help are thought retraining and behavioural exercises.

However, the central common component across most therapies is to enable you to confront your fear by exposing yourself to the situations that you have previously been avoiding. The therapist can use real situations, such as going to the airport, looking at parked aircraft from the outside, stepping inside the aircraft and looking around, taxiing along the runway in a light aircraft, flying in a light aircraft, flying in an airliner under the guidance of the therapist, and finally, flying alone. There are, in addition, other intermediate steps that can be included. When one learns that the predicted terrible consequences, such as the plane falling out of the sky if one does not sit 'lightly' on one's seat, do not arise, the fear begins to diminish, and confidence starts to be built.

Treatments for fear of flying are usually also based on the thoughts that people have about flying, and, as explained, the thought retraining is carried out in three stages. First, the therapist determines which of the client's thoughts about flying are incorrect and increase the fear. Next, the person learns to distance themselves from these thoughts and looks at them critically, as if they were the thoughts of someone else. It then becomes possible for the person to consider whether these thoughts are correct or not, and to learn to think logically about flying on the basis of relevant information.

It has also been proved to be very effective, both in terms of time and costs, to learn to deal with the frightening thoughts and anticipation before the flight, and then a week later to take the flight on a scheduled plane with the therapist, without the requirement of visualization, graded exposure, or relaxation. This forms the basis of the 'Freedom to Fly' course.

As within individual therapy, therapy within a group can also combine the various cognitive behavioural techniques described above. Group therapy works better if it is applied in a number of intensive sessions at short intervals, rather than less intensive sessions spread out over a much longer period. Working in a group has various advantages: the participants quickly see how other people deal with difficult situations, and within the group they are able to overcome their fear of being laughed at, and learn to say out loud what they think. After all, everybody in the group has the same problem. Another advantage is that the participants talk to each other about their problem. By speaking to fellow-sufferers in this way, they come to understand that they are not alone in their fear, and that they are not the only ones with strange, anxious ideas about flying. Very often a spirit of friendly encouragement arises, which can be very positive. The participants are prompted to take steps that they might find much more difficult on their own. Group bonding and a feeling of solidarity develops. When one participant has a particular difficulty, the others spontaneously help them, or encourage them until a positive result is obtained. During the flight, the participants are able to share their impressions and feelings with each other. It is also very moving to be part of a shared success experience. Afterwards, that further step of going on board an aircraft by oneself is not so great, although people sometimes miss the fun and friendship of the group.

Sometimes it can be helpful to use a cabin flight simulator before actually flying. However, very few institutions

153

have access to such an expensive piece of equipment, although some airlines enable courtesy access for therapy. In a simulator, people with fear of flying can experience a complete flight, from beginning to end, in a very realistic way. Another advantage of the simulator is that it is possible for the group to carry out exercises such as flying in their old, accustomed way, and then flying in the new way that they have just learnt, and noting the differences between the two. Despite the fact that whatever level of turbulence or even disaster is simulated and no harm befalls them, it can still be very difficult for some people to enter the simulator, let alone contemplate an aeroplane.

All of the above treatments, whether individual or group-based, should, in our view, be followed by a real flight, under guidance.

It would be interesting to discuss the different treatments in terms of their relative effectiveness, but the published figures are difficult compare because therapists use different criteria to determine whether their treatment is successful or not. In general, however, we can say that both group and individual treatment courses have produced highly successful results, usually in the range of over 90% of people being able to overcome their fears.

Throughout the world, there are an increasing number of treatment opportunities being developed and offered to enable people to overcome their fear of flying. At the third World Congress on Fear of Flying in Montreal in 2007, thirty-five countries participated.

APPENDIX I

WHERE TO OBTAIN THERAPEUTIC HELP

The contact details of the authors are given below. You can also contact them to request details of professional assistance in other countries.

United Kingdom

Freedom to Fly
Elaine Iljon Foreman
Tel: +44 (0)20 8459 3428
E-mail: info@freedomtofly.biz
Website: www.freedomtofly.biz

The Netherlands

The VALK Foundation
Dr Lucas van Gerwen
Postbox 110
2300 AC Leiden
The Netherlands
E-mail: info@valk.org
Tel: +31 71 5273733
Fax: +31 71 5273796
Website: www.valk.org

International reunions on fear of flying

People who have overcome their fear of flying are often keen to share their success stories with others who have done the same. The authors are the first to offer this international opportunity on an annual basis for those who have overcome their difficulties.

People from Freedom to Fly and the VALK Foundation meet up and fly away to a 'foreign land', for a long weekend to celebrate with family and new found friends, their hard won freedom.

The delight in their expanded frontiers can best be summed up in the words of Jonathon Livingston Seagull, from the book by Richard Bach:

'We can be free. We can learn to fly'.

For details, please contact Freedom to Fly or the VALK Foundation at the addresses above.

SELF-EVALUATION: QUESTIONNAIRE 2

You have come to the end of this book and here is the original questionnaire you completed at the start. Please fill it in again. Be honest (again). Show yourself what you are planning to do, and how well informed you now are about the following subjects.

Let us see what has changed.

Circle the appropriate number on the scale, and compare the differences with your first answers at the start of this book.

Not at all————————————Considerably
(0)   (5)

1. How many flights are you planning in the next three years?
   0———1———2———3———4———5
2. How well informed are you about how a plane flies?
   0———1———2———3———4———5
3. How well informed are you about the safety of flying?
   0———1———2———3———4———5
4. How well informed are you about the nature and effects of turbulence?
   0———1———2———3———4———5

5. How well informed are you about the nature and effects of anxiety?

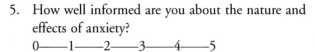

6. How well informed are you about coping strategies to conquer fear of flying?

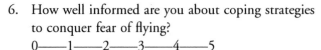

7. How comfortable are you with flying?
   0——1——2——3——4——5

If you would like to participate in our research on the effectiveness of this self-help book, please photocopy and return both questionnaires to:

The VALK Foundation
PO Box 110
2300 AC Leiden
The Netherlands

You can either keep the questionnaire anonymous, or include further comments and your name and address if you wish.

And now it is time to:

Reach for the sky!

FLIGHTS OF FANCY: QUOTATIONS CORNER

Quotable quotes on travel and flight:

People are disturbed not by things, but by the views which they take of them. [Epictetus, 1st century AD]

Nothing is either good or bad, but thinking makes it so. [Shakespeare (*Hamlet*)]

Or, in the night, imagining some fear, how easy is a bush supposed a bear. [Shakespeare (*A Midsummer Night's Dream*)]

The fear of danger is ten times more terrifying than the danger itself. [Daniel Defoe (*Robinson Crusoe*)]

The mind is its own place – and in itself can make a Heaven of Hell or a Hell of Heaven. [Milton (*Paradise Lost*)]

A fear which we are unwilling to face grows worse by not being looked at. [Bertrand Russell]

Nothing in life is to be feared, it is only to be understood. [Marie Curie]

The world is so big, and I am so small, I do not like it at all, at all. [Woodrow Wilson]

Welcome aboard, ladies and gentleman. You have just completed the most dangerous part of your journey –

getting to the airport. [Captain's greetings over the passengers address system]

If man was meant to fly, he would have been born with wings. [Anon]

There are only two emotions in a plane – boredom and panic. [Orson Welles]

On learning to ride a flying machine, if you are looking for perfect safety, you would do well to sit on the fence and watch the birds. But if you wish to learn, you must mount a machine and become acquainted with its tricks by actual trial. [Wilbur Wright, 1901]

Two caterpillars were inching their way through the grass when a butterfly fluttered perilously overhead. They looked up in awe. One caterpillar nudged the other and said, 'You couldn't get me up in one of those things for a million dollars.'

BIBLIOGRAPHY

Iljon Foreman, E. (2003). Putting fear to flight: cases in psychological treatment. In: R. Bor & L. Van Gerwen (Eds.), *Psychological Perspectives on the Fear of Flying* (pp. 229–244). London: Ashgate.

Iljon Foreman, E., Bor, R., & Van Gerwen, L. (2006). Flight or fright? Psychological approaches to the treatment of fear of flying. In: R. Bor & T. Hubbard (Eds.), *Aviation Mental Health* (pp. 69–82). Aldershot: Ashgate.

Van Gerwen, L. J. (1988). *Vliegangst. Verschijnselen, oorzaken en remedie* (*Fear of Flying. Symptoms, Reasons and Remedy*). Baarn, the Netherlands: Ambo.

Van Gerwen, L.J., & Diekstra, R. F. W. (1996). *Help, ik moet vliegen!* (*Help, I Have to Fly!*). Utrecht, the Netherlands: Bruna.

INDEX